Mastering Listening Skills

1

Mastering Listening Skills Book 1

Publisher Chung Kyudo
Editors Kim Jinsuk, Cho Sangik
Author Michael A. Putlack
Designers Yoon Jiyoung, Park Sunyoung

First published in March 2014
By Darakwon, Inc.
Darakwon Bldg., 211, Munbal-ro, Paju-si, Gyeonggi-do 10881
Republic of Korea
Tel: 82-2-736-2031 (Ext. 250)
Fax: 82-2-732-2037

ISBN 978-89-277-0722-6 58740
978-89-277-0721-9 58740 (set)

www.darakwon.co.kr

Components Main Book / Workbook
14 13 12 11 10 9 8 23 24 25 26 27

Mastering Listening Skills

1

DARAKWON

Table of Contents

Introduction

Mastering Listening Skills Book 1 is the third book in a four-book series. This book is intended for intermediate learners of the English language. By using this book, learners will be able to improve their listening skills as well as their knowledge of English.

Mastering Listening Skills Book 1 contains twenty units. The twenty units are divided into five topics, each of which contains four units. The five topics in *Mastering Listening Skills Book 1* are Natural Disasters, Fantasy Worlds, The Roman Era, Art and Artists, and The Environment. These are all topics that young learners find interesting and enjoy learning about. So learners will have fun listening to the material in this book while improving their English at the same time.

Every unit contains one main talk, a shorter talk, and questions about these talks. Each unit also contains a listening skill and exercises on it. The listening skills will help learners improve various aspects of their listening abilities.

Mastering Listening Skills Book 1 has several objectives. First, it will help learners improve their English abilities, particularly their listening skills. Next, it will teach them valuable knowledge about a wide range of academic topics. The talks themselves will also entertain learners as they listen to them. Finally, *Mastering Listening Skills Book 1* will help learners prepare for various standardized tests that they may take in the future. For instance, many questions about the talks are similar to those that appear on the iBT TOEFL® Junior and iBT TOEFL® exams. So, by using this book, learners should be able to get higher scores on the tests they take in the future.

About This Book

There are a total of twenty units. Each unit contains one main talk about a specific topic. There are vocabulary and listening comprehension questions about the main talk. There is also a shorter talk with listening comprehension questions. There are a total of ten listening skills that are taught in the various chapters. Finally, there is a comprehensive vocabulary section as well as a workbook that will help learners increase their understanding of the talks and improve their English abilities.

Unit 01 Krakatoa

Pre-Listening Questions

Answer the following questions.

1 What was Krakatoa?
2 What happened at Krakatoa?
3 What happens when a volcano erupts?
4 Are there any volcanoes in your country? What are they?

Vocabulary

Write the correct word or phrase from the box for each definition.

lava sunset sunrise expel eruption tsunami

1 ________ the exploding of a volcano
2 ________ hot, liquid rock that comes from a volcano
3 ________ to throw out; to cast out
4 ________ the time when the sun goes down
5 ________ the time when the sun goes up
6 ________ a large wave on the ocean that is caused by an earthquake or volcano

Pre-Listening Questions

There are four questions that focus on the picture or pictures at the top of the page. These questions will help prepare learners for the topic of the unit.

Vocabulary

This section contains six vocabulary words from the main talk. Learners should match the words with the definitions.

Talk

This is the main talk of the unit. Each talk is around 250-280 words long and focuses on the topic of the unit.

Organizer

This is a graphic organizer of the talk. There are six blanks for learners to fill in by using words in the talk.

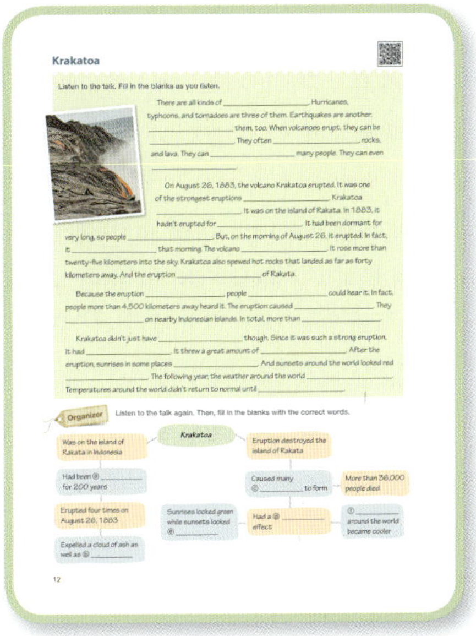

Krakatoa

Listen to the talk. Fill in the blanks as you listen.

Organizer Listen to the talk again. Then, fill in the blanks with the correct words.

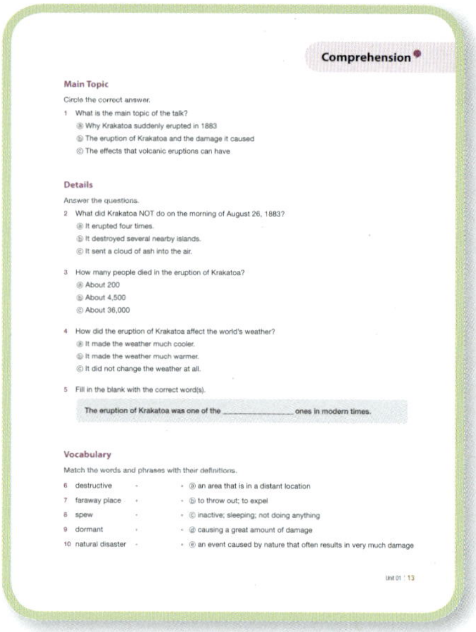
Comprehension

Main Topic

Circle the correct answer.

1 What is the main topic of the talk?
ⓐ Why Krakatoa suddenly erupted in 1883
ⓑ The eruption of Krakatoa and the damage it caused
ⓒ The effects that volcanic eruptions can have

Details

Answer the questions.

2 What did Krakatoa NOT do on the morning of August 26, 1883?
ⓐ It erupted four times.
ⓑ It destroyed several nearby islands.
ⓒ It sent a cloud of ash into the air.

3 How many people died in the eruption of Krakatoa?
ⓐ About 200
ⓑ About 4,500
ⓒ About 36,000

4 How did the eruption of Krakatoa affect the world's weather?
ⓐ It made the weather much cooler.
ⓑ It made the weather much warmer.
ⓒ It did not change the weather at all.

5 Fill in the blank with the correct word(s).

The eruption of Krakatoa was one of the ______________ ones in modern times.

Vocabulary

Match the words and phrases with their definitions.

6 destructive • • ⓐ an area that is in a distant location
7 faraway place • • ⓑ to throw out; to expel
8 spew • • ⓒ inactive; sleeping; not doing anything
9 dormant • • ⓓ causing a great amount of damage
10 natural disaster • • ⓔ an event caused by nature that often results in very much damage

Unit 01 | 13

Comprehension

This page contains several questions about the main talk. There is a question about the main topic or main idea of the talk. There are also four questions that ask about the details in the talk. Finally, there are five vocabulary questions for learners to test their knowledge of the words in the talk.

Listening Skills Practice

This section provides further practice for learners. First, there is a listening skills section in each unit. Various listening skills, such as detail, chronological order, note-taking, dictation, and outlining, are covered in each unit. There is a description of the listening skill as well as questions for learners to test their understanding of the listening skill.

In addition, there is a short talk that is around 150-170 words long. Each talk provides information about a topic related to the main talk. There are comprehension questions and listening skill questions for each short talk as well.

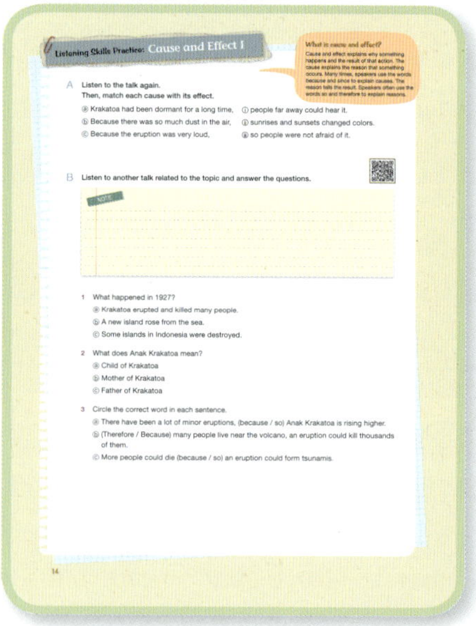
Listening Skills Practice: Cause and Effect I

What is cause and effect?
Cause and effect explains why something happens and the result of that action. The cause explains the reason that something occurs. Many times, speakers use the words because and since to explain causes. The reason tells the result. Speakers often use the words so and therefore to explain reasons.

A Listen to the talk again.
Then, match each cause with its effect.

ⓐ Krakatoa had been dormant for a long time, ⓘ people far away could hear it.
ⓑ Because there was so much dust in the air, ⓙ sunrises and sunsets changed colors.
ⓒ Because the eruption was very loud, ⓚ so people were not afraid of it.

B Listen to another talk related to the topic and answer the questions.

NOTE

1 What happened in 1927?
ⓐ Krakatoa erupted and killed many people.
ⓑ A new island rose from the sea.
ⓒ Some islands in Indonesia were destroyed.

2 What does Anak Krakatoa mean?
ⓐ Child of Krakatoa
ⓑ Mother of Krakatoa
ⓒ Father of Krakatoa

3 Circle the correct word in each sentence.
ⓐ There have been a lot of minor eruptions, (because / so) Anak Krakatoa is rising higher.
ⓑ (Therefore / Because) many people live near the volcano, an eruption could kill thousands of them.
ⓒ More people could die (because / so) an eruption could form tsunamis.

14

Chapter

1

Natural Disasters

Unit 01

Krakatoa

Pre-Listening Questions

Answer the following questions.

1 What was Krakatoa?

2 What happened at Krakatoa?

3 What happens when a volcano erupts?

4 Are there any volcanoes in your country? What are they?

Vocabulary

Write the correct word or phrase from the box for each definition.

lava	sunset	sunrise	expel	eruption	tsunami

1 ____________ the exploding of a volcano

2 ____________ hot, liquid rock that comes from a volcano

3 ____________ to throw out; to cast out

4 ____________ the time when the sun goes down

5 ____________ the time when the sun goes up

6 ____________ a large wave on the ocean that is caused by an earthquake or volcano

Krakatoa

Listen to the talk. Fill in the blanks as you listen.

There are all kinds of ______________________. Hurricanes, typhoons, and tornadoes are three of them. Earthquakes are another. ______________________ them, too. When volcanoes erupt, they can be ______________________. They often ______________________, rocks, and lava. They can ______________________ many people. They can even ______________________.

On August 26, 1883, the volcano Krakatoa erupted. It was one of the strongest eruptions ______________________. Krakatoa ______________________. It was on the island of Rakata. In 1883, it hadn't erupted for ______________________. It had been dormant for very long, so people ______________________. But, on the morning of August 26, it erupted. In fact, it ______________________ that morning. The volcano ______________________. It rose more than twenty-five kilometers into the sky. Krakatoa also spewed hot rocks that landed as far as forty kilometers away. And the eruption ______________________ of Rakata.

Because the eruption ______________________, people ______________________ could hear it. In fact, people more than 4,500 kilometers away heard it. The eruption caused ______________________. They ______________________ on nearby Indonesian islands. In total, more than ______________________.

Krakatoa didn't just have ______________________ though. Since it was such a strong eruption, it had ______________________. It threw a great amount of ______________________. After the eruption, sunrises in some places ______________________. And sunsets around the world looked red ______________________. The following year, the weather around the world ______________________. Temperatures around the world didn't return to normal until ______________________.

Organizer Listen to the talk again. Then, fill in the blanks with the correct words.

Krakatoa

- Was on the island of Rakata in Indonesia
- Had been ⓐ __________ for 200 years
- Erupted four times on August 26, 1883
- Expelled a cloud of ash as well as ⓑ __________
- Eruption destroyed the island of Rakata
- Caused many ⓒ __________ to form
- More than 36,000 people died
- Had a ⓓ __________ effect
- Sunrises looked green while sunsets looked ⓔ __________
- ⓕ __________ around the world became cooler

Comprehension

Main Topic

Circle the correct answer.

1 What is the main topic of the talk?

ⓐ Why Krakatoa suddenly erupted in 1883

ⓑ The eruption of Krakatoa and the damage it caused

ⓒ The effects that volcanic eruptions can have

Details

Answer the questions.

2 What did Krakatoa NOT do on the morning of August 26, 1883?

ⓐ It erupted four times.

ⓑ It destroyed several nearby islands.

ⓒ It sent a cloud of ash into the air.

3 How many people died in the eruption of Krakatoa?

ⓐ About 200

ⓑ About 4,500

ⓒ About 36,000

4 How did the eruption of Krakatoa affect the world's weather?

ⓐ It made the weather much cooler.

ⓑ It made the weather much warmer.

ⓒ It did not change the weather at all.

5 Fill in the blank with the correct word(s).

The eruption of Krakatoa was one of the ________________ ones in modern times.

Vocabulary

Match the words and phrases with their definitions.

6 destructive	ⓐ an area that is in a distant location
7 faraway place	ⓑ to throw out; to expel
8 spew	ⓒ inactive; sleeping; not doing anything
9 dormant	ⓓ causing a great amount of damage
10 natural disaster	ⓔ an event caused by nature that often results in very much damage

Listening Skills Practice: Cause and Effect I

What is cause and effect?

Cause and effect explains why something happens and the result of that action. The cause explains the reason that something occurs. Many times, speakers use the words *because* and *since* to explain causes. The reason tells the result. Speakers often use the words *so* and *therefore* to explain reasons.

A **Listen to the talk again.**
Then, match each cause with its effect.

ⓐ Krakatoa had been dormant for a long time,
ⓑ Because there was so much dust in the air,
ⓒ Because the eruption was very loud,

ⓘ people far away could hear it.
ⓘⓘ sunrises and sunsets changed colors.
ⓘⓘⓘ so people were not afraid of it.

B **Listen to another talk related to the topic and answer the questions.**

NOTE

1 What happened in 1927?

ⓐ Krakatoa erupted and killed many people.
ⓑ A new island rose from the sea.
ⓒ Some islands in Indonesia were destroyed.

2 What does Anak Krakatoa mean?

ⓐ Child of Krakatoa
ⓑ Mother of Krakatoa
ⓒ Father of Krakatoa

3 Circle the correct word in each sentence.

ⓐ There have been a lot of minor eruptions, (because / so) Anak Krakatoa is rising higher.
ⓑ (Therefore / Because) many people live near the volcano, an eruption could kill thousands of them.
ⓒ More people could die (because / so) an eruption could form tsunamis.

Unit 02 The San Francisco Earthquake

Pre-Listening Questions

Answer the following questions.

1 What can you see in the pictures?

2 What do you think happened?

3 What is an earthquake?

4 Have you ever been in an earthquake? What was it like?

Vocabulary

Write the correct word or phrase from the box for each definition.

suffer	aftershock	population	coast	measure	destruction

1 ____________ the number of people living in a certain area

2 ____________ a great amount of damage

3 ____________ to determine how big, heavy, or long something is

4 ____________ to experience something bad or harmful

5 ____________ a small earthquake that happens after a large one

6 ____________ a place next to a large body of water

The San Francisco Earthquake

Listen to the talk. Fill in the blanks as you listen.

San Francisco is a city in ____________________ of California. In 1906, it was the largest city on ____________________. It was also ____________________ in the country. More than 400,000 people lived in San Francisco. In addition to ____________________, it was also ____________________ in the United States.

Then, at 5:12 AM on April 18, 1906, disaster struck. ____________________ the city. An earthquake happens when ____________________. This earthquake was very strong. It lasted ____________________. People as far away as Los Angeles ____________________ the earthquake. It measured between 7.7 and 7.9 on the Richter scale.

Since the earthquake was so strong, it caused ____________________ damage. ____________________ buildings were destroyed. There were also ____________________. These are weaker earthquakes that ____________________. They ____________________ to the city.

However, the earthquake didn't cause ____________________. Instead, a fire caused the most destruction. The earthquake ____________________ in San Francisco. So ____________________ from these damaged lines. Then, ____________________. It lasted ____________________. By the time it ended, it had affected a huge part of the city.

Around 3,000 people probably died because of ____________________. In addition, more than ____________________ after these two disasters. That was half of ____________________. The city suffered ____________________ in damage. The San Francisco Earthquake was one of ____________________ ever to affect the United States.

Organizer Listen to the talk again. Then, fill in the blanks with the correct words.

The San Francisco Earthquake

- Happened at 5:12 AM on April 18, ⓐ __________
- Lasted for nearly ⓑ __________ minute
- Measured between 7.7 and 7.9 on the Richter scale
- Were many ⓒ __________

- Caused a great deal of ⓓ __________
- Damaged some ⓔ __________
  - Resulted in a fire that lasted for four days
- About 3,000 people ⓕ __________ due to the earthquake and fire
- More than 200,000 people became homeless

Comprehension

Main Topic

Circle the correct answer.

1 What is the main idea of the talk?

ⓐ The San Francisco Earthquake caused a lot of death and destruction.

ⓑ The worst natural disaster in history was the San Francisco Earthquake.

ⓒ The San Francisco Earthquake lasted for almost one minute.

Details

Answer the questions.

2 About how many people lived in San Francisco in 1906?

ⓐ 3,000

ⓑ 200,000

ⓒ 400,000

3 What did NOT happen after the San Francisco Earthquake?

ⓐ Many buildings were destroyed.

ⓑ A big fire burned a large part of the city.

ⓒ There were aftershocks stronger than the first earthquake.

4 Which statement about the San Francisco Earthquake is true?

ⓐ Around 30,000 people died because of it.

ⓑ Half of the city's population became homeless after it.

ⓒ It killed more people than any other natural disaster.

5 Fill in the blank with the correct word(s).

A big ________________ caused more damage in San Francisco than the earthquake did.

Vocabulary

Match the words and phrases with their definitions.

6 gas line	ⓐ a system that measures the strength of earthquakes
7 last	ⓑ lacking a permanent place to live
8 tremor	ⓒ an earthquake
9 Richter scale	ⓓ to go on in time
10 homeless	ⓔ a pipe that carries gas

Listening Skills Practice: Cause and Effect II

What is cause and effect?

Cause and effect explains why something happens and the result of that action. The cause explains the reason that something occurs. The reason tells the result. The cause and effect often appear in the same sentence. Other times, they appear in two different sentences. Pay close attention so that you can find both of them.

A **Listen to the talk again.**
Then, match each cause with its effect.

ⓐ The earthquake damaged some gas lines,	ⓘ so the ground began to move.
ⓑ There was an earthquake,	ⓘⓘ people in Los Angeles felt it.
ⓒ Because the earthquake was very strong,	ⓘⓘⓘ so many small fires started.

B **Listen to a school report related to the topic and answer the questions.**

NOTE

1 What did the New Madrid Earthquake measure on the Richter scale?

ⓐ Around 7.0

ⓑ Around 8.0

ⓒ Around 9.0

2 What happened after the New Madrid Earthquake?

ⓐ Large cities were destroyed.

ⓑ Some new lakes formed.

ⓒ Several rivers were created.

3 Circle the correct word in each sentence.

ⓐ (So / Because) there is a fault in the Earth's crust, earthquakes can happen there.

ⓑ The earthquake was very powerful, (so / because) the Mississippi River began to flow north.

ⓒ Only a few people were killed (so / because) not many people lived in the area.

Unit 03

The Tunguska Event

Pre-Listening Questions

Answer the following questions.

1 What do you think happened in the pictures?

2 How big are some asteroids and comets?

3 If an asteroid or comet hits the Earth, what can it do?

4 Do you know of any asteroid or comet strikes on the Earth? What happened?

Vocabulary

Write the correct word or phrase from the box for each definition.

rare	speck	latter	explode	diameter	estimate

1 ____________ the second of two

2 ____________ to blow up

3 ____________ uncommon; not usual

4 ____________ the width of a circular object

5 ____________ to make a guess about something

6 ____________ something very tiny, such as a grain of sand

The Tunguska Event

Listen to the talk. Fill in the blanks as you listen.

Every day, thousands of meteors enter the Earth's atmosphere. Most are ____________________. Others are no larger than ____________________. At times, rocks the size of a baseball or basketball enter the Earth's atmosphere. Most of these meteors ____________________. Those are the streaks of light we see in the night sky. ____________________, large meteors not only enter the Earth's atmosphere, but they ____________________. They may hit the ground. Or they may ____________________. The latter happened in Tunguska, Russia, many years ago.

Tunguska is ____________________ in Siberia, Russia. Most people around the world had ____________________. That changed ____________________, 1908, though. On that morning, ____________________ the Earth's atmosphere. ____________________ it was between fifty and ____________________. It probably weighed more than one hundred million kilograms. And it was moving around ____________________.

Between five and ten kilometers ____________________, the meteor exploded. The explosion was 1,000 times more powerful than ____________________ on Hiroshima, Japan, during World War II. Fortunately, the meteor exploded ____________________ with few people. The explosion ____________________ in a region covering more than 2,000 square kilometers. When ____________________, it became ____________________.

This became known as the Tunguska Event. It showed people ____________________. If the meteor had hit ____________________, millions of people would have died. So now many astronomers spend time looking for ____________________.

Organizer Listen to the talk again. Then, fill in the blanks with the correct words.

Meteors

- ⓐ __________ enter Earth's atmosphere daily
- May be very small or the size of a ball
- Sometimes ⓑ __________ the ground or explode near the ground
- Usually burn up so look like ⓒ __________ of light

The Tunguska Event

- Happened on June 30, 1908, near Tunguska, ⓓ __________
- Was caused by a large meteor between 50-200 meters in diameter
- Destroyed most of the ⓔ __________ in a large area
- Was ⓕ __________ more times powerful than an atomic bomb

Comprehension

Main Topic

Circle the correct answer.

1 What is the main idea of the talk?

ⓐ No one knows how big the meteor that caused the Tunguska Event was.

ⓑ The Tunguska Event showed the power of meteors when they hit the Earth.

ⓒ The most powerful meteor ever to crash into the Earth hit at Tunguska, Russia.

Details

Answer the questions.

2 What do most meteors do when they enter the Earth's atmosphere?

ⓐ They explode.

ⓑ They hit the ground.

ⓒ They burn up.

3 Where is Tunguska?

ⓐ Russia

ⓑ Canada

ⓒ China

4 What is NOT true about the Tunguska Event?

ⓐ The meteor destroyed many trees.

ⓑ Many people died because of the meteor.

ⓒ The explosion was brighter than the sun.

5 Fill in the blank with the correct word(s).

Some ________________ meteors may explode near the ground or hit the ground.

Vocabulary

Match the words and phrases with their definitions.

6 remote area	•	• ⓐ a region with many trees
7 forested area	•	• ⓑ to explode; to go off; to detonate
8 populated region	•	• ⓒ an area with people in it
9 blow up	•	• ⓓ a powerful explosive that uses the power of the atom
10 atomic bomb	•	• ⓔ a place far away

Listening Skills Practice: Connecting Words I

What are connecting words?

Connecting words combine two or more words, sentences, and phrases. Use connecting words to put similar facts and opinions together. Or use them to make comparisons and contrasts. A connecting word often appears at the beginning of *a sentence. And, but, or, when, then, in addition*, and *however* are some common connecting words.

A **Listen to the talk again. Then, use the connecting words in the box to complete the sentences.**

And	When	But

ⓐ Most meteors are very small. ________________ some meteors can be much larger.

ⓑ ________________ the meteor entered the Earth's atmosphere, it was moving around 20,000 kilometers per hour.

ⓒ The explosion destroyed most of the trees in the region. ________________ it was brighter than the sun.

B **Listen to another talk related to the topic and answer the questions.**

NOTE

1 About how big was the crater that hit the Yucatan Peninsula?

ⓐ It was about 10 meters wide.

ⓑ It was about 100 meters wide.

ⓒ It was about 10 kilometers wide.

2 What happened after the asteroid hit the ground?

ⓐ It caused some powerful snowstorms.

ⓑ All life on the planet died.

ⓒ A lot of dust went into the air.

3 Choose the correct connecting words for the sentences.

ⓐ Sixty-five million years ago, the dinosaurs died. (But / Then), the age of mammals began.

ⓑ A lot of dust went into the air, (however / so) this kept the sun from shining on the planet.

ⓒ The dinosaurs died (when / and) the weather became very cold.

Unit 04 The Southeast Asian Tsunami

Pre-Listening Questions

Answer the following questions.

1 What can you see in the picture on the left?

2 What do you think happened in the picture on the right?

3 What is a tsunami?

4 What do you know about the Southeast Asian Tsunami?

Vocabulary

Write the correct word or phrase from the box for each definition.

destructive	suffer	village	inland	recede	donate

1 ____________ a small town

2 ____________ to give money, goods, or time to others

3 ____________ away from water; away from a coast

4 ____________ causing a lot of damage

5 ____________ to go back

6 ____________ to experience pain or harm

The Southeast Asian Tsunami

Listen to the talk. Fill in the blanks as you listen.

Earthquakes don't just happen on land. They ____________________. When there's a big underwater earthquake, it can affect ____________________. An underwater tremor can create a tsunami. A tsunami can ____________________. It starts as a very fast-moving wave of water. But, as it approaches shore, ____________________. The water near shore recedes away from the coast. It can go back hundreds of meters. Then, as the tsunami ____________________, it slows down. The water that recedes becomes a part of the tsunami. This increases the size of the wave. So ____________________ may hit land. Some tsunamis can be ____________________. They can also go far inland.

On December 26, 2004, there was a major tsunami. In the morning, ____________________ took place in the Indian Ocean. It ____________________ on the Richter scale. It created ____________________ all over the Indian Ocean. At least ____________________ were hit by tsunamis. Some were ____________________. Others were enormous.

Many towns, villages, and cities along the coast ____________________. More than 230,000 people ____________________. At least one million people lost their homes. Indonesia ____________________. More than ____________________ there. Thousands of people also died in Thailand, Sri Lanka, and India. In addition, ____________________ and have never ____________________ again.

Thankfully, ____________________ billions of dollars in aid after the tsunami. The recovery was difficult in many countries. But ____________________ helped the survivors try to ____________________.

Organizer Listen to the talk again. Then, fill in the blanks with the correct words.

Tsunamis

- Are caused by ⓐ __________ earthquakes
- Are destructive, ⓑ __________ waves
- Increases the ⓒ __________ of the wave
- Water ⓓ __________ when tsunami gets near shore

The Southeast Asian Tsunami

- Happened on December 26, ⓔ __________
- Was caused by a 9.0 earthquake in the Indian Ocean
- More than 230,000 people died and others lost their ⓕ __________
- Hit 18 countries in the area

Comprehension

Main Topic

Circle the correct answer.

1 What is the main topic of the talk?

ⓐ A tsunami that killed many people

ⓑ How tsunamis form

ⓒ Earthquakes in Southeast Asia

Details

Answer the questions.

2 What happens when a tsunami gets near shore?

ⓐ The wave becomes bigger.

ⓑ It starts to move faster.

ⓒ It loses a lot of water.

3 Where did the underwater earthquake take place?

ⓐ In the Pacific Ocean

ⓑ In the Antarctic Ocean

ⓒ In the Indian Ocean

4 Which country was NOT affected by the Southeast Asian Tsunami?

ⓐ Thailand

ⓑ Japan

ⓒ Indonesia

5 Fill in the blank with the correct word(s).

> **More than 230,000 people died, and around one ________________ people became homeless because of the tsunami.**

Vocabulary

Match the words and phrases with their definitions.

6	aid	ⓐ to be completely destroyed
7	be wiped out	ⓑ help; assistance
8	incredibly	ⓒ a person who lives through a bad event
9	survivor	ⓓ very; extremely; highly
10	fast-moving	ⓔ swift; quick

Listening Skills Practice: Connecting Words II

What are connecting words?

Connecting words combine two or more words, sentences, and phrases. Use connecting words to put similar facts and opinions together. Or use them to make comparisons and contrasts. Many times, connecting words are in the middle of a sentence. Some common connecting words are *and*, *but*, *so*, *as*, *when*, and *because*.

A **Listen to the talk again. Then, use the connecting words in the box to complete the sentences.**

so	as	and

ⓐ A tsunami slows down ________________ it gets closer to land.

ⓑ A powerful underwater earthquake took place, ________________ it caused a tsunami.

ⓒ People donated money to the survivors, ________________ they tried to get their lives back together.

B **Listen to a news broadcast related to the topic and answer the questions.**

Memo

1 Where did the tsunamis hit Japan?

ⓐ On the west coast

ⓑ On the east coast

ⓒ On the south coast

2 What are officials very worried about?

ⓐ A nuclear reactor

ⓑ Some skyscrapers

ⓒ Tokyo

3 Choose the correct connecting words for the sentences.

ⓐ The earthquake registered 9.0, (so / but) it was one of the strongest earthquakes in history.

ⓑ Many coastal towns suffered damage (but / and) so did many villages.

ⓒ Thousands of people may have died, (so / and) a huge number of homes and buildings have been destroyed.

Chapter

2

Fantasy Worlds

Unit 05

Narnia

Pre-Listening Questions

Answer the following questions.

1 What are the titles of the books about Narnia?

2 What kind of land is Narnia?

3 How would you like to be in a land with talking animals?

4 What are some other fantasy worlds that you know about?

Vocabulary

Write the correct word or phrase from the box for each definition.

dryad	witch	faun	wardrobe	somehow	feature

1 ____________ in some way

2 ____________ to star; to be about

3 ____________ a female tree spirit

4 ____________ a large piece of furniture that is used to hold clothes

5 ____________ a woman who can do magic

6 ____________ a creature that is half man and half goat

Narnia

Listen to the talk. Fill in the blanks as you listen.

One day, four children are playing in big house. The children's names are Peter, Susan, Edmund, and Lucy. They open __________ and discover __________. The name of this world is Narnia. It's __________ much different from ours. For example, many of the animals in Narnia can speak. There are __________, and other animals. Numerous creatures __________ live there, too. There are fauns, centaurs, and dryads as well as __________.

The children find out that Narnia is in the middle of __________. The White Witch has created __________. She is __________ of Narnia. Fortunately, Aslan is in Narnia. He is the great lion, the son of the Emperor-Over-The-Sea, and __________. The children then meet Aslan, fight the White Witch, and __________. After that, they __________ of Narnia.

This is the story of *The Lion, the Witch, and the Wardrobe*. It was __________ C.S. Lewis. *The Lion, the Witch, and the Wardrobe* is the first book of *The Chronicles of Narnia*. It is also __________ of the books about Narnia. There are __________. All seven of the books __________ from our world who __________ to Narnia. There, they have all kinds of __________.

The Chronicles of Narnia are some of __________ children's books in the world. They have sold __________. Some movies __________ have become very popular as well.

Organizer Listen to the talk again. Then, fill in the blanks with the correct words.

Narnia

- Is a ⓐ __________ world with talking animals
- Has creatures from mythology and monsters
- 4 children and ⓑ __________ defeat the White Witch and then become kings and queens
- Is in a 100-year-long winter because of the ⓒ __________

The Chronicles of Narnia

- Was written by C.S. Lewis
- Contains ⓓ __________ books
- Features children and their adventures in ⓔ __________
- First book is *The Lion, the Witch, and* ⓕ __________

Comprehension

Main Topic

Circle the correct answer.

1 What is the main topic of the talk?

ⓐ The story of Peter, Susan, Edmund, and Lucy

ⓑ *The Chronicles of Narnia*

ⓒ Aslan and the animals of Narnia

Details

Answer the questions.

2 Why is there a 100-year-long winter in Narnia?

ⓐ Because of the centaurs

ⓑ Because of Aslan

ⓒ Because of the White Witch

3 Which of the following is NOT true of Aslan?

ⓐ He is the true ruler of Narnia.

ⓑ He is a great lion.

ⓒ He is the Emperor-Over-The-Sea.

4 What is the first book in *The Chronicles of Narnia*?

ⓐ *Prince Caspian*

ⓑ *The Horse and His Boy*

ⓒ *The Lion, the Witch, and the Wardrobe*

5 Fill in the blank with the correct word(s).

Narnia is a fantasy world with ________________ animals, creatures from mythology, and terrible monsters.

Vocabulary

Match the words and phrases with their definitions.

6 fantasy world •	• ⓐ a creature with the body of a horse but the upper body of a man
7 chronicle •	• ⓑ favorite; liked very much; adored
8 centaur •	• ⓒ to learn; to discover
9 find out •	• ⓓ an imaginary world in which magic exists
10 beloved •	• ⓔ a story; a history

Listening Skills Practice: Details I

What are details?

Use details to learn the facts in a talk. A talk can have many kinds of details. They can be names, dates, and places. They can be statements of fact. They can provide reasons why certain events occur. They can also give the results of certain events.

A Listen to the talk again. Then, write the correct details in the blanks.

ⓐ Four children open the door to a ________________ and discover the fantasy world ________________ inside it.

ⓑ The children meet ________________, fight the White Witch and her army, and then become the ________________ of Narnia.

ⓒ There are ________________ books in *The Chronicles of Narnia*, and the most popular book is ________________.

B Listen to another talk related to the topic and answer the questions.

NOTE

1 What is Mr. Tumnus?

ⓐ A centaur

ⓑ A talking mouse

ⓒ A faun

2 Which book does Reepicheep NOT appear in?

ⓐ *The Lion, the Witch, and the Wardrobe*

ⓑ *The Last Battle*

ⓒ *The Voyage of the Dawn Treader*

3 Write T (true) or F (false) for the following statements about characters in the Narnia books.

ⓐ ________ Mr. Tumnus and Lucy become good friends.

ⓑ ________ Reepicheep is the leader of the White Witch's army.

ⓒ ________ Reepicheep is brave and willing to fight.

Unit 06

Middle-Earth

Pre-Listening Questions

Answer the following questions.

1 What can you see in the pictures above?

2 Have you read *The Lord of the Rings* books or seen the movies? How were they?

3 What kind of fantasy land is Middle-earth?

4 What kinds of creatures live in Middle-earth?

Vocabulary

Write the correct word or phrase from the box for each definition.

decade	awful	elf	quest	trilogy	fearsome

1 ____________ a period of ten years

2 ____________ a mission; a goal to find or do something

3 ____________ terrible; horrible

4 ____________ frightening; scary

5 ____________ a group of three books or movies that are related to one another

6 ____________ a magical creature that resembles a human

Middle-Earth

Listen to the talk. Fill in the blanks as you listen.

As a young boy, J.R.R. Tolkien studied ____________________. The knowledge he gained from his studies later helped him ____________________ Middle-earth.

Tolkien wrote about Middle-earth over a period of decades. It is a land with ____________________. There are humans. Elves and dwarves live there, too. The elves ____________________ while the dwarves live ____________________. There are ____________________ Ents as well as awful monsters such as orcs. Great and powerful wizards ____________________. Finally, there are hobbits. They are ____________________ that lived in a part of Middle-earth called the Shire.

Tolkien wrote several books that ____________________. One was called *The Silmarillion*. Tolkien wrote it first, but it was published ____________________. It tells the story of ____________________ of Middle Earth. In 1937, he published *The Hobbit*. This was ____________________ based in Middle-earth. The book is about ____________________ Bilbo Baggins. He, a group of dwarves, and the wizard Gandalf ____________________ to kill a fearsome dragon.

____________________ based in Middle-earth are the three books that make up *The Lord of the Rings* trilogy. They tell the story of ____________________ the One Ring. The books feature Gandalf and other wizards. There are hobbits, elves, dwarves, and men. There are ____________________ and monsters. The books tell an epic tale of ____________________. They have been popular ____________________, and it's likely that ____________________ far into the future.

Organizer Listen to the talk again. Then, fill in the blanks with the correct words.

Middle-Earth

- Was created by J.R.R. Tolkien
- Has humans, elves, and ⓐ __________
- Are also Ents, ⓑ __________, and wizards
- Has hobbits, which live in the ⓒ __________

- *The Silmarillion* tells about the ⓓ __________ of Middle-earth
- *The Hobbit* is about a quest to kill a ⓔ __________
- *The Lord of the Rings* books are the most famous
  - Tell an ⓕ __________ of good overcoming evil

Comprehension

Main Topic

Circle the correct answer.

1 What is the main idea of the talk?

ⓐ Many people love reading *The Lord of the Rings* books.

ⓑ Hobbits are an important race in Middle-earth.

ⓒ J.R.R. Tolkien wrote many books set in Middle-earth.

Details

Answer the questions.

2 Which of the following does NOT live in Middle-earth?

ⓐ Fairies

ⓑ Elves

ⓒ Hobbits

3 What is the goal in *The Hobbit*?

ⓐ To find the One Ring

ⓑ To kill a dragon

ⓒ To fight the dwarves

4 What is true about *The Lord of the Rings* books?

ⓐ They are the best-known books about Middle-earth.

ⓑ They were written before *The Hobbit*.

ⓒ They tell the story of the creation of Middle-earth.

5 Fill in the blank with the correct word(s).

***The Hobbit* tells the tale of Bilbo Baggins, a group of dwarves, and the ________________ Gandalf.**

Vocabulary

Match the words and phrases with their definitions.

6	overcome	ⓐ to defeat; to beat; to win against
7	epic tale	ⓑ resembling humans
8	best-known	ⓒ a man who can use magic
9	wizard	ⓓ a long story that is about great deeds
10	humanlike	ⓔ most famous

Listening Skills Practice: Details II

What are details?

Use details to learn the facts in a talk. A talk can have many kinds of details. These details provide important information about the topic of the talk. They often answer questions that begin with wh-question words such as *who*, *what*, *when*, *where*, *how*, and *why*.

A **Listen to the talk again. Then, write the correct details in the blanks.**

ⓐ In Middle-earth, ________________ live in the forests while dwarves live ________________.

ⓑ *The Silmarillion* tells about the ________________ of Middle-earth, but it was published after Tolkien ________________.

ⓒ ________________ trilogy is about a ________________ to destroy the One Ring and has been popular for decades.

B **Listen to a movie review related to the topic and answer the questions.**

NOTE

1 Which of the following is NOT in *The Lord of the Rings* trilogy?

ⓐ *The Fellowship of the Ring*

ⓑ *The Two Towers*

ⓒ *The Hobbit*

2 What does the student think of the movie *The Return of the King*?

ⓐ He did not really enjoy it.

ⓑ He thinks it was excellent.

ⓒ He believes it could be better.

3 Write T (true) or F (false) for the following statements about *The Return of the King*.

ⓐ ________ It is the second movie in *The Lord of the Rings* trilogy.

ⓑ ________ It tells about the quest to destroy the One Ring.

ⓒ ________ It is very different from the book *The Return of the King*.

Unit **07**

The Magical World of Oz

Pre-Listening Questions

Answer the following questions.

1 Who are the main characters in *The Wizard of Oz*?

2 What else do you know about Oz?

3 Have you ever seen the movie *The Wizard of Oz*? How was it?

4 What other fantasy movies have you seen?

Vocabulary

Write the correct word or phrase from the box for each definition.

star	tiny	tornado	immediate	pleased	eventually

1 ____________ very small

2 ____________ instant

3 ____________ a twister; a small windstorm that moves very quickly

4 ____________ to be the main character in

5 ____________ happy

6 ____________ after a long time

The Magical World of Oz

Listen to the talk. Fill in the blanks as you listen.

In 1939, a movie starring Judie Garland came out. ______________, it wasn't very successful. Later, it was rereleased and ______________. Then, in the 1950s, the film ______________ every year. Over time, it became one of ______________ in the world. The title of the movie was *The Wizard of Oz*.

The movie ______________ *The Wonderful Wizard of Oz*. It was written by Frank Baum in 1900. In the story, Dorothy ______________ in Kansas. One day, there's a tornado. Dorothy and her dog Toto ______________, but the tornado ______________ the house and ______________. Eventually, the house ______________ of Oz.

There are all kinds of ______________. First, Dorothy meets ______________ called the Munchkins. She learns that ______________ the Wicked Witch of the East and ______________. So the Munchkins ______________ Dorothy. Dorothy, however, only wants to go home. She learns that she ______________ the Emerald City. There, she can speak with the Wizard of Oz, who can help her.

______________ the Emerald City, Dorothy makes friends with the Scarecrow, the Tin Woodman, and ______________. They have many adventures together in Oz. For instance, they have to ______________ as well as the Wicked Witch of the West. Eventually, Dorothy and Toto ______________ Kansas.

The Wonderful Wizard of Oz was ______________. It was so popular that Baum wrote ______________ that took place in the fantasy land ______________.

Organizer Listen to the talk again. Then, fill in the blanks with the correct words.

The Wonderful Wizard of Oz

- Was a book written by Frank Baum in ⓐ __________
- Made into the ⓑ __________ *The Wizard of Oz* in 1939
- Began airing every year in the 1950s
- Became one of the ⓒ __________ movies

- Dorothy and Toto are taken to Oz by a ⓓ __________
- Must go to the Emerald City
- Meet the ⓔ __________, the Tin Woodman, and the Cowardly Lion
- ⓕ __________ get back to Kansas

Comprehension

Main Topic

Circle the correct answer.

1 What is the main idea of the talk?

ⓐ Dorothy and Toto have adventures in the fantasy land of Oz.

ⓑ Frank Baum wrote the book *The Wonderful Wizard of Oz*.

ⓒ Dorothy made friends with four creatures in the movie.

Details

Answer the questions.

2 How does Dorothy arrive in Oz?

ⓐ A witch casts a spell on her.

ⓑ She walks there.

ⓒ A tornado takes her there.

3 Who is happy to meet Dorothy?

ⓐ The Munchkins

ⓑ The Wicked Witch of the East

ⓒ The Wizard of Oz

4 Who does Dorothy NOT make friends with?

ⓐ The Cowardly Lion

ⓑ The Winged Monkeys

ⓒ The Tin Woodman

5 Fill in the blank with the correct word(s).

Dorothy and Toto go to the ____________________ to speak with the Wizard of Oz.

Vocabulary

Match the words and phrases with their definitions.

6	make friends with •	• ⓐ a big success
7	pick up •	• ⓑ to lift
8	hit •	• ⓒ to handle; to do something about
9	deal with •	• ⓓ the name of a book, printed work, or movie
10	title •	• ⓔ to become friends with

Listening Skills Practice: Inference I

What is inference?

Inference involves learning information that is not directly mentioned by the speakers. Speakers often imply certain facts. They do this by speak indirectly. They give hints about certain things that they do not mention directly. Listen carefully. Then, you can understand what the speakers are implying.

A **Listen to the talk again. Then, choose the correct inferences.**

ⓐ *The Wizard of Oz* became one of the most beloved movies in the world.
- ⓘ People in many countries have seen *The Wizard of Oz*.
- ⓘⓘ Lots of people think *The Wizard of Oz* is boring.

ⓑ Dorothy's house kills the Wicked Witch of the East. The Munchkins are pleased to meet Dorothy.
- ⓘ The Munchkins miss the Wicked Witch of the East.
- ⓘⓘ The Munchkins disliked the Wicked Witch of the East.

ⓒ Dorothy makes friends with the Scarecrow, the Tin Woodman, and the Cowardly Lion. Eventually, Dorothy and Toto make it back to Kansas.
- ⓘ The Scarecrow goes to Kansas with Dorothy.
- ⓘⓘ Dorothy's friends stay in Oz.

B **Listen to another talk related to the topic and answer the questions.**

NOTE

1 What can be inferred the people in Earthsea?
- ⓐ They can all use magic.
- ⓑ They are afraid of dragons.
- ⓒ They mostly live near water.

2 What can be dangerous in Earthsea?
- ⓐ Telling people one's name
- ⓑ Trying to use magic
- ⓒ Sailing on the oceans

3 What can be inferred about Ged?
- ⓐ He fights a dragon in one book.
- ⓑ He is the greatest wizard in Earthsea.
- ⓒ He appears in several novels.

Unit 08

The World of *Harry Potter*

Pre-Listening Questions

Answer the following questions.

1 Who is Harry Potter?

2 Have you read any of the *Harry Potter* books or seen the movies? How did you like them?

3 Who are some of the people in the world of *Harry Potter*?

4 What else do you know about the world of *Harry Potter*?

Vocabulary

Write the correct word or phrase from the box for each definition.

event	enemy	ability	imagine	series	wizard

1 ____________ to think of something that does not exist or has not happened

2 ____________ a hated or disliked opponent

3 ____________ a male who can use magic

4 ____________ a skill; a talent

5 ____________ an action; something that happens

6 ____________ a group of things that are related to one another

The World of *Harry Potter*

Listen to the talk. Fill in the blanks as you listen.

Imagine that some people in our world ____________________. They ____________________. Instead, they ____________________ to do all sorts of things. Not only that, but there are also ____________________, elves, and goblins. There are magical items, too. And there's ____________________ between good wizards and witches and evil ones as well. That's the world of *Harry Potter*.

Harry Potter is one of the most successful ____________________ ever. There are seven books ____________________. They were written by J.K. Rowling. They've sold ____________________ more than 450 million copies. There are ____________________ in the franchise. The movies have made ____________________ in sales around the world.

The books and movies follow ____________________ and his friends. The events in each book take ____________________. The first book is *Harry Potter and the Sorcerer's Stone*. In it, Harry finds out that ____________________. He begins taking classes at a school of magic called Hogwarts. He ____________________ such as Ron, Hermione, and Hagrid while he's at school. He also ____________________ such as Draco Malfoy.

In each book, Harry must battle ____________________ Lord Voldemort. In some cases, he actually has to fight Voldemort, ____________________ wizard in the world, himself. Thanks to ____________________ as well as the skills of his friends, Harry ____________________ these encounters. The battles aren't easy though, and sometimes his friends and family members die. In the last book, called *Harry Potter and the Deathly Hallows*, he ____________________ Voldemort.

Organizer Listen to the talk again. Then, fill in the blanks with the correct words.

Harry Potter

- Is a world with magic, magical creatures, and ⓐ __________
- Are ⓑ __________ books and eight movies
- Is a very successful franchise

- Follow the ⓒ __________ of Harry Potter and his friends
- Makes friends and enemies at ⓓ __________
- Must fight the ⓔ __________ wizard Voldemort
- ⓕ __________ thanks to his abilities

Main Topic

Circle the correct answer.

1 What is the main topic of the talk?

ⓐ The amount of money *Harry Potter* has made

ⓑ The events in the *Harry Potter* books and movies

ⓒ The characters in the world of *Harry Potter*

Details

Answer the questions.

2 What is NOT correct about the *Harry Potter* franchise?

ⓐ It was created by J.K. Rowling.

ⓑ There are eight books in the series.

ⓒ The movies have made almost eight billion dollars.

3 What is the title of the first Harry Potter book?

ⓐ *Harry Potter and the Sorcerer's Stone*

ⓑ *Harry Potter and the Chamber of Secrets*

ⓒ *Harry Potter and the Deathly Hallows*

4 What is true about Lord Voldemort?

ⓐ He fights Harry Potter in every book.

ⓑ He is an evil wizard.

ⓒ He kills most of Harry Potter's friends.

5 Fill in the blank with the correct word(s).

There are ________________ people, creatures, and items in the world of *Harry Potter*.

Vocabulary

Match the words and phrases with their definitions.

6	battle	ⓐ ability; a talent
7	all sorts of	ⓑ 1,000,000,000
8	evil	ⓒ very bad; wicked
9	skill	ⓓ to fight
10	billion	ⓔ all kinds of; a variety of

Listening Skills Practice: Inference II

What is inference?

Inference involves learning information that is not directly mentioned by the speakers. Many talks contain implied statements. So the speakers do not directly state information. Instead, they imply it. Listen carefully to the statements the speakers make. Try to infer information from them.

A Listen to the talk again. Then, choose the correct inferences.

ⓐ There are eight *Harry Potter* movies. The movies have made nearly eight billion dollars in sales around the world.
  ⓘ People in only a few countries have seen the movies.
  ⓘⓘ The movies were successful all around the world.

ⓑ In *Harry Potter and the Sorcerer's Stone*, Harry finds out that he is a wizard.
  ⓘ Harry was an outstanding wizard as a child.
  ⓘⓘ Harry did not know any wizards before that time.

ⓒ Harry manages to win each encounter with Voldemort. In *Harry Potter and the Deathly Hallows*, he has his final fight with Voldemort.
  ⓘ Harry defeats Voldemort in the final fight.
  ⓘⓘ Voldemort defeats Harry in the final fight.

B Listen to a talk by a bookstore employee related to the topic and answer the questions.

Memo

1 What can be inferred about *The Dresden Files*?
  ⓐ They have sold a lot of copies.
  ⓑ They are nonfiction books.
  ⓒ They have been made into movies.

2 What is NOT true about Harry Dresden?
  ⓐ He is a wizard who lives in Chicago.
  ⓑ He works as a detective.
  ⓒ He is often considered an outsider.

3 What can be inferred about Jim Butcher?
  ⓐ He will write at least five more books about Harry Dresden.
  ⓑ He has written some other series of books.
  ⓒ He works as a detective in his free time.

Chapter

3

The Roman Era

Unit 09

Romulus and Remus

Pre-Listening Questions

Answer the following questions.

1 What can you see in the picture?

2 What do you know about the founding of Rome?

3 Who are some famous people from Roman history?

4 Does your country have any myths about its foundation? What are they?

Vocabulary

Write the correct word or phrase from the box for each definition.

she-wolf	riverbank	shepherd	seize	twins	argue

1 __________ the side of a river

2 __________ to grab; to take

3 __________ to fight, often with words

4 __________ a female wolf

5 __________ two children born to the same mother at the same time

6 __________ a person who takes care of sheep

Romulus and Remus

Listen to the talk. Fill in the blanks as you listen.

For nearly 1,000 years, Rome was among the most powerful cities in the world. It was ______________ both the Roman Republic and ______________. According to legend, it was founded ______________ The Romans had ______________ the founding of their city. It ______________ Romulus and Remus.

There was once a city in central Italy called Alba Longa. The king of Alba Longa was Numitor. He ______________ Rhea Silvia. One day, Numitor's brother Amulius ______________ Numitor. He ______________ and sent Rhea away. Sometime later, Rhea became pregnant. She ______________. Their names were Romulus and Remus. And their father was Mars, ______________.

Amulius found out about Rhea's children. So he had them ______________. The basket was set in the Tiber River, and ______________. However, the basket ______________. There, a she-wolf found the twins. She protected them and ______________. A woodpecker ______________. Later, ______________ found the twins and raised them.

The twins eventually learned ______________. They worked together to kill Amulius. They ______________. They didn't want to wait to ______________ from their grandfather. So they decided to ______________. They discovered a place by the Tiber River ______________. It was the perfect spot. But the twins argued over which hill they should build their city on. They ______________, and Romulus killed Remus. Romulus then built the city, ______________.

Organizer Listen to the talk again. Then, fill in the blanks with the correct words.

Romulus and Remus

- Amulius seized the ⓐ __________ of Alba Longa from Numitor
- Rhea Silvia had ⓑ __________ Romulus and Remus
- Twins were ⓒ __________ a she-wolf and raised by shepherds
- Twins ⓓ __________ Amulius and decided to found a city

- Found a place with ⓔ __________
- Romulus killed Remus
- Romulus founded Rome
- Rome became a powerful city for ⓕ __________ years

Main Topic

Circle the correct answer.

1 What is the main topic of the talk?

ⓐ The myth of Romulus and Remus
ⓑ The first years of the city of Rome
ⓒ The lives of Numitor and Rhea

Details

Answer the questions.

2 Who was Numitor?

ⓐ The son of Rhea Silvia
ⓑ The king of Alba Longa
ⓒ The founder of Rome

3 Which animal did NOT help Romulus and Remus?

ⓐ A woodpecker
ⓑ A wolf
ⓒ A bear

4 What happened when Romulus and Remus had an argument?

ⓐ They decided to found Rome together.
ⓑ Romulus killed Remus in a fight.
ⓒ Remus returned to Alba Longa.

5 Fill in the blank with the correct word(s).

The myth of Romulus and Remus is the story of the ________________ of Rome.

Vocabulary

Match the words and phrases with their definitions.

6 give birth to • • ⓐ to receive something from one's parents after they die
7 found • • ⓑ to make a person go somewhere else
8 inherit • • ⓒ to have a child
9 send away • • ⓓ to establish; to start a city, company, or group
10 float off • • ⓔ to drift away on water

Listening Skills Practice: Chronological Order I

What is chronological order?

Chronological order is a way to put events in order. Talks do not always include days, dates, and times. In those cases, remember the order of the events in the talk. Then, put them in the exact order in which they occurred in the talk.

A **Listen to the talk again. Then, put the sentences into chronological order.**

ⓐ ________ A she-wolf found Romulus and Remus and took care of them.

ⓑ ________ Amulius seized the throne of Alba Longa from Numitor.

ⓒ ________ Romulus killed Remus in a fight and then founded Rome.

B **Listen to another talk related to the topic and answer the questions.**

NOTE

1 Which poem was written by Virgil?

ⓐ The *Iliad*

ⓑ The *Aeneid*

ⓒ The *Odyssey*

2 What was Aeneas's destiny?

ⓐ To marry Queen Dido of Carthage

ⓑ To start the city of Troy

ⓒ To be the father of a powerful race of people

3 Listen to the talk again. Then, put the sentences into chronological order.

ⓐ ________ Queen Dido fell in love with Aeneas.

ⓑ ________ Aeneas sailed to Italy and landed there.

ⓒ ________ Aeneas and his followers escaped from Troy.

Unit 10 The Roman Republic

Pre-Listening Questions

Answer the following questions.

1 What can you see in the pictures?

2 When was the Roman Republic?

3 What do you know about the Roman Republic?

4 What was life like in your country a long time ago?

Vocabulary

Write the correct word or phrase from the box for each definition.

territory	elect	legend	peasant	monarchy	represent

1 ____________ a government in which a king is the top person

2 ____________ a poor person who is often a farmer

3 ____________ a story from the past that may or may not be true

4 ____________ to act in place of another person or people

5 ____________ land controlled by a country

6 ____________ to choose a person for a position

The Roman Republic

Listen to the talk. Fill in the blanks as you listen.

According to legend, Rome was founded in 753 B.C. ______________ was Romulus, the city's founder. For around 240 years, Rome ______________. However, some Romans decided that they didn't want to be ruled by kings. So the wealthy aristocrats and ______________. They ______________. In 509 B.C., Rome ______________.

A republic is ______________ representative government. The Romans ______________ in the Roman Senate. These senators represented ______________. Over time, the Romans developed ______________. This helped ______________.

Because Rome was united, it ______________. The Romans began to ______________. The Roman army ______________ throughout the Italian peninsula. This happened around 400 B.C. ______________, Rome ruled ______________.

That was also the year that the First Punic War began. As Rome ______________, it ______________ other powers in the Mediterranean region. One was Carthage. Carthage ______________ North Africa. Rome ______________ Carthage. Rome won the Third Punic War ______________ and destroyed Carthage. This ______________ of the Mediterranean region to Rome.

Rome's territory quickly expanded. It ______________ that are modern-day Spain, France, and Greece. It ruled land ______________ and Northern Africa, too. Eventually, though, some of ______________ in Rome fought one another. This ______________. The Roman Republic ended in 27 B.C. when Augustus Caesar ______________. This started the time of ______________.

Organizer **Listen to the talk again. Then, fill in the blanks with the correct words.**

The Roman Republic

- Was ruled by kings from 753 B.C. to 509 B.C.
- Became a ⓐ __________ in 509 B.C.
- Had a form of ⓑ __________ government
- Ruled most of Italian peninsula by 264 B.C.

- First Punic War against Carthage started in ⓒ __________
- Destroyed ⓓ __________ after Third Punic War in 146 B.C.
- Expanded territory in ⓔ __________, Africa, and Middle East
- Was a civil war so ended in 27 B.C. when Augustus Caesar became ⓕ __________

Main Topic

Circle the correct answer.

1 What is the main idea of the talk?

ⓐ The Roman Republic grew to be very strong over the years.

ⓑ The Roman Republic was established in 509 B.C.

ⓒ Rome defeated Carthage in three separate wars.

Details

Answer the questions.

2 What is a republic?

ⓐ It is a government ruled by a king.

ⓑ It is a type of representative government.

ⓒ It is a government ruled by the wealthy.

3 Which of the following is NOT true of the Punic Wars?

ⓐ Rome and Carthage fought them.

ⓑ The first one began in 264 B.C.

ⓒ Carthage won the Third Punic War.

4 What caused the end of the Roman Republic?

ⓐ Rome's territories in the Middle East rebelled.

ⓑ The Roman people demanded to have a king.

ⓒ There was a civil war between powerful men.

5 Fill in the blank with the correct word(s).

Rome was ____________________ in 753 B.C. and lasted as a republic until 27 B.C.

Vocabulary

Match the words and phrases with their definitions.

6 wealthy aristocrat •	• ⓐ a rich nobleman
7 peninsula •	• ⓑ to start to fight
8 expand •	• ⓒ to grow in size
9 come into conflict with •	• ⓓ to make secure or normal
10 stabilize •	• ⓔ land with water on three sides

Listening Skills Practice: Chronological Order II

What is chronological order?
Chronological order is a way to put events in order. Chronological order refers to time. Many times, the speaker mentions days, years, dates, and times. In that case, listen carefully to the talk. Listen for the important dates and numbers. Use this information to put the events in the talk in the correct chronological order.

A Listen to the talk again. Then, put the sentences in chronological order.

ⓐ ________ The Roman people got rid of the monarchy and started a republic.

ⓑ ________ There was a civil war in Rome, and Rome became an empire.

ⓒ ________ Rome defeated Carthage in the Third Punic War.

B Listen to a student give a report related to the topic and answer the questions.

NOTE

1 What did Cincinnatus prefer to do?
ⓐ Spend time on his farm
ⓑ Speak in the Senate
ⓒ Lead a Roman army

2 Why was Cincinnatus a great Roman?
ⓐ He defeated a powerful army.
ⓑ He willingly gave up power.
ⓒ He founded the Roman Republic.

3 Write the correct years or numbers in the blanks. Then, put the sentences into chronological order.

ⓐ ________ Cincinnatus won the war and gave up power ________________ days after getting it.

ⓑ ________ In ________________, the Roman Senate made Cincinnatus a dictator.

ⓒ ________ In ________________, Cincinnatus was a consul in Rome.

Unit 11

Julius Caesar

Pre-Listening Questions

Answer the following questions.

1 Who was Julius Caesar?

2 How did Julius Caesar die?

3 What else do you know about Julius Caesar's life?

4 Do you know any other famous Romans? What did they do?

Vocabulary

Write the correct word or phrase from the box for each definition.

beat	senator	plot	orator	corruption	stab

1 ____________ to defeat; to win against

2 ____________ fraud; dishonesty; illegal actions, often by people in the government

3 ____________ to make a plan against another person

4 ____________ a public speaker

5 ____________ to cut with a knife, sword, or other sharp weapon

6 ____________ a member of a senate; a high-level elected person in a representative government

Julius Caesar

Listen to the talk. Fill in the blanks as you listen.

Julius Caesar was ____________ of the Roman Republic. He ____________ several fields. He was a lawyer and orator. Some said ____________ Cicero's. Cicero was considered ____________. Caesar held many positions in the government. He was a talented writer. And he was ____________.

Julius Caesar was born in 100 B.C. When he was growing up, the Roman Republic had ____________. There was ____________. This caused the republic ____________. After becoming an adult, Caesar ____________ several government positions. He fought corruption. He ____________ for the Senate to pass. He also tried to help the poor people in Rome have better lives.

When he was forty-one, he ____________ Gaul. Gaul was the ancient name of France. In Gaul, Caesar ____________ a Roman army. He ____________ in Gaul. He ____________. Tribes from Germany and other areas attacked his armies. But Caesar ____________. By then, he had become one of ____________.

As Caesar gained more power, the Roman Senate ____________. The senators feared Caesar ____________. They were right. In 49 B.C., Caesar ____________. He ____________. Most of the poor people were happy. But the senators were upset. Caesar made lots of changes in Rome. Many senators ____________. So some of them ____________ Caesar. On March 15, 44 B.C., several men ____________ and killed him when he entered the Senate.

Organizer Listen to the talk again. Then, fill in the blanks with the correct words.

Julius Caesar

- Was born in 100 B.C.
- Was ⓐ ____________ in several fields
- Fought ⓑ ____________ as an elected official
- Fought many battles while he was in Gaul

- Entered Rome with his army and ⓒ ____________
- Made many ⓓ ____________
- Senators ⓔ ____________ him
- Stabbed Caesar and killed him on ⓕ ____________, 44 B.C.

Comprehension

Main Topic

Circle the correct answer.

1 What is the main topic of the talk?

ⓐ The military actions of Julius Caesar

ⓑ The fall of the Roman Republic

ⓒ The life and actions of Julius Caesar

Details

Answer the questions.

2 Which statement about Julius Caesar is NOT correct?

ⓐ He was a better orator than Cicero.

ⓑ He was an excellent general.

ⓒ He was a good writer.

3 Where did Julius Caesar fight many battles?

ⓐ In Germany

ⓑ In Gaul

ⓒ In Rome

4 Who was upset when Julius Caesar took power in Rome?

ⓐ The poor

ⓑ Some senators

ⓒ The people in Rome's colonies

5 Fill in the blank with the correct word(s).

> **Julius Caesar was stabbed and ________________ in the Senate on March 15, 44 B.C.**

Vocabulary

Match the words and phrases with their definitions.

6	general	ⓐ to become stronger
7	gain power	ⓑ to be talented; to be skilled
8	be accomplished	ⓒ to lose power, strength, or ability
9	be in charge of	ⓓ the leader of an army; a high-ranking military officer
10	go into decline	ⓔ to be the leader of someone or something

Listening Skills Practice: Problem and Solution I

What is problem and solution?

Problem and solution can show what is wrong and how someone fixes the problem. Many speakers talk about various problems. They also usually describe one or more solutions to each problem. Listen carefully to identify both the problems and solutions in a talk.

A **Listen to the talk again. Then, write P (problem) or S (solution).**

ⓐ ________ There was a lot of government corruption.

ⓑ ________ Many senators disliked Julius Caesar as the leader of the government.

ⓒ ________ Some senators plotted to kill Julius Caesar.

B **Listen to another talk related to the topic and answer the questions.**

NOTE

1 Which person was NOT a member of the Second Triumvirate?

ⓐ Octavian

ⓑ Mark Antony

ⓒ Julius Caesar

2 What happened at the Battle of Actium?

ⓐ Octavian killed Mark Antony and Cleopatra.

ⓑ Octavian's forces defeated Mark Antony and Cleopatra.

ⓒ The army of Lepidus was defeated.

3 Listen to the talk again. Then, write the solution for each problem.

ⓐ There was a struggle for power in Rome.

____

ⓑ Mark Antony needed an ally.

____

Unit 12 The Fall of the Roman Empire

Pre-Listening Questions

Answer the following questions.

1 When did the Roman Empire fall?

2 Who defeated the Roman Empire?

3 Why did the Roman Empire fall?

4 What else do you know about the Roman Empire?

Vocabulary

Write the correct word or phrase from the box for each definition.

tribe	big	split	antiquity	steal	politician

1 ____________ to take something from someone else

2 ____________ important; major

3 ____________ a group of people who are similar to one another

4 ____________ a government official

5 ____________ to divide into two

6 ____________ a time long ago in the past; ancient times

The Fall of the Roman Empire

Listen to the talk. Fill in the blanks as you listen.

The Roman Empire started in 27 B.C. It ____________________ During that time, Rome expanded a great deal. ____________________, it controlled most of ____________________, parts of Britain, and much of North Africa and ____________________. It was ____________________ in antiquity. And Rome was the world's most important city.

All empires eventually fall though. This ____________________ Rome. Rome ____________________ for several reasons. A big reason involved Emperor Diocletian. In 285, he decided that the Roman Empire was ____________________ for one person to rule. So he ____________________. He created the Western Roman Empire and the Eastern Roman Empire. ____________________ in the west. The capital in the east became Constantinople. Much of Rome's wealth went east. This ____________________.

At the same time, ____________________ in the west gained power. These tribes included the Visigoths, Vandals, and Franks. They ____________________ the Roman legions. This caused the Western Roman Empire ____________________. The politicians in Rome were ____________________, too. They ____________________ to improve their own lives. Doing that ____________________ to Rome.

In 410, a Germanic army of Visigoths ____________________. The army destroyed lots of buildings and ____________________. Rome wasn't captured though. Then, in 476, another Germanic army attacked Rome. The army's leader was Odoacer. His army captured Rome. Odoacer made Emperor Romulus Augustulus ____________________. He was ____________________. So historians say that the fall of the Roman Empire ____________________.

Organizer Listen to the talk again. Then, fill in the blanks with the correct words.

The Decline of Rome

- Diocletian split the empire into ⓐ __________ parts
- Much of Rome's ⓑ __________ went to the east
- ⓒ __________ in Rome were weak and corrupt
- ⓓ __________ tribes in the west defeated Roman legions

The Fall of Rome

- Visigoths invaded Rome in ⓔ __________
- Odoacer and his army attacked Rome in 476
- Was the last Roman emperor, so the empire ⓕ __________ then
- Emperor Romulus Augustulus gave up the throne

Main Topic

Circle the correct answer.

1 What is the main idea of the talk?

ⓐ Odoacer and his army captured Rome.

ⓑ The fall of Rome happened in 476.

ⓒ Many factors led to the fall of Rome.

Details

Answer the questions.

2 What did Emperor Diocletian do?

ⓐ He founded the city of Constantinople.

ⓑ He split the Roman Empire into two parts.

ⓒ He gave up the throne as emperor.

3 Which of the following was NOT a barbarian tribe in the west?

ⓐ The Visigoths

ⓑ The Mongols

ⓒ The Franks

4 When did the Roman Empire fall?

ⓐ 285

ⓑ 410

ⓒ 476

5 Fill in the blank with the correct word(s).

The last ________________ of the Roman Empire was Romulus Augustulus.

Vocabulary

Match the words and phrases with their definitions.

6 harm •	• ⓐ damage; injury
7 legion •	• ⓑ very much; a lot
8 be the case •	• ⓒ to step down as king; to quit serving as king
9 give up the throne •	• ⓓ to be true; to happen in reality
10 a great deal •	• ⓔ a Roman army

Listening Skills Practice: Problem and Solution II

What is problem and solution?

Problem and solution can show what is wrong and how someone fixes the problem. In most talks, the speaker mentions the problem first. Then, the speaker talks about the solution or solutions to the problem. Many times, the speaker talks about the solution more than the problem.

A Listen to the talk. Then, write P (problem) or S (solution).

ⓐ ________ Emperor Diocletian split the Roman Empire into two halves.

ⓑ ________ The Roman Empire was impossible for one man to rule.

ⓒ ________ The politicians in Rome were weak and corrupt.

B Listen to a report by a student related to the topic and answer the questions

NOTE

1 Who was the first Byzantine Emperor?

ⓐ Diocletian

ⓑ Constantine

ⓒ Justinian

2 What happened in 1453?

ⓐ The Ottoman Turks captured Constantinople.

ⓑ The Byzantine Empire rejoined the Roman Empire.

ⓒ Constantinople's name changed to Istanbul.

3 Listen to the talk again. Then, write the solution for each problem.

ⓐ Constantine had no capital city when he became the emperor.

____

ⓑ The Muslims were attempting to get into Europe.

____

C h a p t e r

4

Art and Artists

Unit 13

Realism

Pre-Listening Questions

Answer the following questions.

1 What kind of art is Realism?

2 When was the Realism Period?

3 Who were some artists in the Realism Period?

4 What other artists do you know? What kind of art did they make?

Vocabulary

Write the correct word or phrase from the box for each definition.

everyday	reaction	precisely	landscape	complain	detest

1 ____________ usual; normal

2 ____________ to hate; to dislike very much

3 ____________ exactly

4 ____________ a response to someone or something

5 ____________ to talk negatively about someone or something

6 ____________ a painting that shows a nature scene

Realism

Listen to the talk. Fill in the blanks as you listen.

At the end of the 1700s, ____________________. People called it ____________________. It influenced many different fields, including art. The art of the Romantic Era ____________________. Imagination and mystery were also important to the art of this time. The Romantic Era lasted until the mid-1800s. By then, artists ____________________. They wanted to create ____________________.

This new style was called Realism. It lasted from about 1840 to 1880. Realism ____________________ Romanticism. So the two styles of art were very different. First of all, Realist artists ____________________. They tried to paint their subjects ____________________ in real life. Next, Realist artists painted pictures of ____________________. For example, they painted farmers working in their fields. Others painted people eating food or ____________________ in them. Realist artists didn't have ____________________ in their art. They simply wanted to show the world as it existed.

There were ____________________ from this time. Gustave Courbet was one. Honore Daumier and Winslow Homer were two others. The Realist Era lasted for ____________________. But it wasn't popular with everyone. ____________________ that the scenes were ugly. They thought Realist artists didn't make the people in their paintings look good. The upper class ____________________. Realist paintings ____________________ the members of ____________________ were. Yet many other people liked the art of this era. Today, paintings from that period ____________________.

Organizer Listen to the talk again. Then, fill in the blanks with the correct words.

Realism

- Lasted from 1840 to ⓐ __________
- Was a ⓑ __________ to the Romantic Movement
- Subjects were painted precisely as they looked in ⓒ __________
- Painted ⓓ __________ people and events

- Included Gustave Courbet, Honore Daumier, and ⓔ __________
- Was disliked by art critics and the ⓕ __________
- Others liked the paintings of the era very much

Comprehension

Main Topic

Circle the correct answer.

1 What is the main idea of the talk?

ⓐ Realist art was different from Romantic art.

ⓑ Realism involved artist painting everyday scenes as they really looked.

ⓒ A lot of art critics and members of the upper class disliked Realism.

Details

Answer the questions.

2 When did the Realist Period last?

ⓐ From 1780 to 1840

ⓑ From 1840 to 1880

ⓒ From 1880 to 1910

3 What did Realist artists NOT paint?

ⓐ Landscapes with animals

ⓑ People eating food

ⓒ Scenes from mythology

4 Which statement about Realism is correct?

ⓐ Most art critics of the time loved Realist paintings.

ⓑ The members of the lower classes enjoyed Realist art.

ⓒ Winslow Homer painted in the Realist style.

5 Fill in the blank with the correct word(s).

Realist art began as a reaction to the ________________ Movement.

Vocabulary

Match the words and phrases with their definitions.

6	influence •	• ⓐ the poor members of society
7	upper class •	• ⓑ to affect; to have an effect on
8	lower class •	• ⓒ a person who comments on art
9	pay attention to •	• ⓓ to watch closely; to listen to closely
10	art critic •	• ⓔ the rich members of society

Listening Skills Practice: Summarizing I

What is summarizing?

Summarizing can help you find the main idea of a talk. To summarize a talk, forget about the minor details and unimportant information in the talk. Think about the main theme of the talk. Try to make one sentence out of that theme. That is the summary sentence.

A Listen to the talk again. Then, choose the correct summary sentence.

ⓐ Realist artists painted everyday scenes with great detail.

ⓑ Gustave Courbet and Honore Daumier were two Realist artists.

ⓒ The Realist Period and Romantic Period were different from each other.

B Listen to another talk related to the topic and answer the questions.

NOTE

1 What was the Salon?

ⓐ It was the official art exhibition in France.

ⓑ It was a French art school.

ⓒ It was the most important museum in France.

2 Which of the following did the Impressionists NOT use?

ⓐ Broad brushstrokes

ⓑ Bright colors

ⓒ Dark backgrounds

3 Choose the correct summary sentence.

ⓐ The Salon rejected several of Edouard Manet's paintings.

ⓑ Edouard Manet created art in both the Realist and Impressionist styles.

ⓒ Edouard Manet painted a lot of art that showed everyday scenes.

Unit 14

Dutch Golden Age Painting

Pre-Listening Questions

Answer the following questions.

1 When was the Dutch Golden Age?

2 Why did the Dutch people have a golden age?

3 Who were some Dutch artists from that time?

4 What kinds of paintings do you think artists made during the Dutch Golden Age?

Vocabulary

Write the correct word or phrase from the box for each definition.

etching	enormous	incredibly	patron	prolific	wealthy

1 ____________ a person who sponsors or pays for another person to do something

2 ____________ huge; very large

3 ____________ the act of making art on a metal or glass plate by using acid

4 ____________ productive; creating very much of something

5 ____________ extremely

6 ____________ rich

Dutch Golden Age Painting

Listen to the talk. Fill in the blanks as you listen.

In the 1600s, England, France, and Spain were ____________________. Another much smaller country was also a great power. This country was the Netherlands. The Netherlands, or Holland, is a small country ____________________. It lies to the west of Germany and ____________________. To the north is the North Sea. In the 1600s, the Netherlands was ____________________. Despite only having two million people, the Dutch had ____________________. Due to their enormous wealth, many Dutch people ____________________. This led to a period called Dutch Golden Age Painting.

During the 1600s, Dutch artists were very prolific. ____________________ that Dutch artists created ____________________ during this period. Dutch artists made ____________________. They often focused on ____________________, and genre paintings. Genre paintings show ____________________. Other Dutch artists painted ____________________.

____________________ from this time was Rembrandt. He painted hundreds of paintings and also ____________________. He made all kinds of paintings, including ____________________. His paintings are ____________________ and tend to ____________________. *Christ in the Storm* and *The Blinding of Samson* are two of his ____________________. *The Night Watch* is another famous painting by Rembrandt. Jan Vermeer was another great artist from that time. He ____________________ than Rembrandt, but art historians still call him ____________________. Frans Hals and Jan Steen were two other noted artists from this time.

Organizer Listen to the talk again. Then, fill in the blanks with the correct words.

The Dutch Golden Age

- Happened in the ⓐ ____________
- ⓑ ____________ was a global power
- Thanks to wealth, many Dutch became ⓒ ____________ of the arts
- The Netherlands was wealthy and powerful

Dutch Golden Age Art

- Made up to ⓓ ____________ million paintings of various types
- Made portraits, still-lifes, ⓔ ____________, historical scenes, and landscapes
- Other great artists were Vermeer, Hals, and Steen
- ⓕ ____________ was the most famous artist

Comprehension

Main Topic

Circle the correct answer.

1 What is the main topic of the talk?

ⓐ The art of the Dutch Golden Age

ⓑ The Dutch Empire in the 1600s

ⓒ Rembrandt's and Vermeer's art

Details

Answer the questions.

2 Why did many Dutch people become patrons of the arts?

ⓐ They wanted to own many pictures.

ⓑ They were interested in learning to paint.

ⓒ They had large amounts of money.

3 Around how many paintings did Dutch artists create during the 1600s?

ⓐ Three million

ⓑ Four million

ⓒ Five million

4 Which of the following paintings did Rembrandt NOT paint?

ⓐ *The Night Watch*

ⓑ *Starry Night*

ⓒ *Christ in the Storm*

5 Fill in the blank with the correct word(s).

Many art historians today say that Jan Vermeer was a ________________.

Vocabulary

Match the words and phrases with their definitions.

6 global empire •	• ⓐ a great painter
7 master painter •	• ⓑ a painting of objects that do not move
8 art historian •	• ⓒ an empire that is spread around the world
9 striking •	• ⓓ impressive
10 still-life •	• ⓔ a person who studies art

Listening Skills Practice: Summarizing II

What is summarizing?

Summarizing can help you determine the main point of a talk. To summarize a talk, forget about the minor details and unimportant information. Think about the main theme from the talk. Then, make a summary sentence that uses some of the key words from the talk.

A **Listen to the talk again. Then, choose the correct summary sentence.**

ⓐ Many Dutch artists painted portraits, but others made different paintings.

ⓑ Rembrandt and Vermeer were the best two Dutch painters.

ⓒ The Dutch Golden Age was a prolific period for Dutch artists.

B **Listen to a talk by a documentary narrator related to the topic and answer the questions.**

Memo

1 About how many drawing did Rembrandt make?

ⓐ 600

ⓑ 1,600

ⓒ 2,000

2 Which statement about *The Night Watch* is true?

ⓐ It is Rembrandt's most famous work.

ⓑ It is a very large painting.

ⓒ It was the first painting Rembrandt made.

3 Choose the correct summary sentence.

ⓐ Some of Rembrandt's paintings were large while others were small.

ⓑ Rembrandt was a great artist who made art in many different genres.

ⓒ The program is going to talk about the life of Rembrandt.

Unit 15

Frederic Remington

Pre-Listening Questions

Answer the following questions.

1 What can you see in the pictures above?

2 Who was Frederic Remington?

3 What kind of art do you think he made?

4 What type of art do you enjoy?

Vocabulary

Write the correct word or phrase from the box for each definition.

sketching	unsettled	ranching	untamed	watercolor	sculpture

1 __________ farming involving keeping large herds of animals such as cows or sheep

2 __________ drawing

3 __________ a kind of water-based paint

4 __________ not lived in; having no people living in it

5 __________ wild

6 __________ a statue

Frederic Remington

Listen to the talk. Fill in the blanks as you listen.

In the 1800s, ____________________ east of the Mississippi River. The western part of the country was ____________________. It was ____________________. There were lots of wild animals such as grizzly bears, ____________________. There were Indians who often made ____________________. The West was also ____________________ in the eastern part of the country.

One of the people ____________________ was Frederic Remington. Born in 1861, he ____________________ to the West when he was ____________________. Remington enjoyed ____________________. He liked ____________________. He tried ranching out West. He was also an artist.

____________________, Remington began sketching and drawing pictures of scenes in the West. He ____________________ to the magazine *Harper's Weekly*. They were ____________________. The American public ____________________ the pictures. They wanted more. Remington quickly realized he could ____________________ being an artist.

Remington created ____________________. He painted with ____________________. He drew pictures. And he made sculptures as well. He used the ____________________ for his work. He often created artwork ____________________. He made many pictures of the U.S. Cavalry as well. His works often showed the scenery of the American West as well. One of his most famous works was the sculpture *The Bronco Buster*. It shows ____________________ that's standing on ____________________. He made ____________________. One of the original sculptures is in the Oval Office in ____________________.

Organizer Listen to the talk again. Then, fill in the blanks with the correct words.

The American West
- Was mostly ⓐ ____________ in the 1800s
- Was an untamed and dangerous land
- Was ⓑ ____________ to people in the East
- Had ⓒ ____________ and Indians that fought wars

Frederic Remington
- Enjoyed outdoor activities and the American West
- Sold pictures to *Harper's Weekly* that were ⓓ ____________
- Most famous work is *The Bronco Buster*
- Painted with watercolors and oils, drew pictures, and made ⓕ ____________
- Made art with cowboys, ⓔ ____________, U.S. Cavalry, and western scenery

Main Topic

Circle the correct answer.

1 What is the main topic of the talk?

ⓐ The life and work of Frederic Remington

ⓑ The American West in the 1800s

ⓒ The best artwork of Frederic Remington

Details

Answer the questions.

2 What was the American West like in the 1800s?

ⓐ It was full of many settlers.

ⓑ It was dangerous yet had many people.

ⓒ It was a dangerous and unsettled land.

3 Which kind of art did Frederic Remington NOT make?

ⓐ Drawings

ⓑ Photographs

ⓒ Sculptures

4 What is *The Bronco Buster*?

ⓐ It is a sculpture of a man on a horse.

ⓑ It is a painting of the U.S. Cavalry.

ⓒ It is a drawing of cowboys and Indians.

5 Fill in the blank with the correct word(s).

Frederic Remington enjoyed ________________ such as hunting, fishing, and hiking.

Vocabulary

Match the words and phrases with their definitions.

6 cowboy •	• ⓐ very interesting
7 cavalry •	• ⓑ a group of soldiers on horseback
8 settler •	• ⓒ to be very interested in
9 fascinating •	• ⓓ a man who works on a ranch and takes care of cows
10 be intrigued by •	• ⓔ a person who moves to live in a land with few people in it

Listening Skills Practice: Note-Taking I

What is note-taking?

Note-taking is a way to organize and write down important information in a talk. Do not write complete sentences while taking notes. Instead, listen carefully to the speaker. Focus on the key words and phrases the person says. Write down the important information by using short phrases and words. Ignore minor points and unimportant information.

A Circle the important words and phrases in each sentence.

ⓐ The western part of the country was mostly unsettled. It was an untamed, dangerous land.

ⓑ In his early twenties, Remington began sketching and drawing pictures of scenes in the West.

ⓒ He painted with both watercolors and oils. He drew pictures. And he made sculptures as well.

B Listen to another talk related to the topic and answer the questions.

NOTE

1 What kind of artist was Ansel Adams?

ⓐ A photographer

ⓑ A painter

ⓒ A sculptor

2 What is Yosemite?

ⓐ A park in San Francisco

ⓑ An American national park

ⓒ The biggest park in California

3 Listen to the talk again. Take notes on the following topics.

ⓐ photography: ______________________

ⓑ Yosemite: ______________________

ⓒ Ansel Adam's photography: ______________________

Unit 16

Vincent van Gogh

Pre-Listening Questions

Answer the following questions.

1 What do you know about the pictures?

2 Who was Vincent van Gogh?

3 What kind of art did he paint?

4 Who are some of your favorite artists?

Vocabulary

Write the correct word or phrase from the box for each definition.

genius	productive	major	vibrant	masterpiece	period

1 ____________ a certain time in history

2 ____________ a very intelligent or talented person

3 ____________ lively; energetic

4 ____________ a great work or art, music, or literature

5 ____________ doing a great amount of work

6 ____________ important; significant

Vincent van Gogh

Listen to the talk. Fill in the blanks as you listen.

One of history's greatest artists __________ during his entire life. And he sold that painting just __________ before he died. During his life, his paintings were __________. His brother even owned an art gallery and tried to sell the paintings. __________ purchasing them. After he died, though, people __________ his work. They realized that this man had been __________. Today, his paintings sell for millions of dollars. The name of this artist is Vincent van Gogh.

Van Gogh had __________. He often had __________. As a result, he had to __________. He battled __________ for much of his life. This caused him to __________ and to commit suicide when he was __________. He also had little formal training as an artist.

Still, he loved drawing and painting. During his life, he was __________. He created more than __________ in his life. Around 900 of them were paintings. He sometimes completed masterpieces __________. Van Gogh's first major work was __________. He finished it in 1885. That was from his first period as an artist. *The Potato Eaters* used __________. But van Gogh's style changed later in his life. He began painting with __________. He used this style for his painting *Starry Night*. It is one of __________ works of art in the world. Van Gogh painted it in 1889. A year later, in 1890, he killed himself, and the art world lost a genius.

Organizer Listen to the talk again. Then, fill in the blanks with the correct words.

Vincent van Gogh's Life

- Had little or no ⓐ __________ so borrowed from others
- Battled ⓑ __________ for much of his life
- Cut off part of his ear and killed himself in 1890
- Only sold ⓒ __________ painting during his life

Vincent van Gogh's Art

- Created more than 2,000 works of art, including ⓓ __________ paintings
- *The Potato Eaters* was his first ⓔ __________ work
- Most famous painting is ⓕ __________
- Used both very dark colors and vibrant bright colors

Main Topic

Circle the correct answer.

1 What is the main idea of the talk?

ⓐ Vincent van Gogh was a great, productive artist.

ⓑ Vincent van Gogh killed himself at a young age.

ⓒ Vincent van Gogh only sold one painting during his life.

Details

Answer the questions.

2 Which statement about Vincent van Gogh is true?

ⓐ He sold many paintings from his brother's art gallery.

ⓑ He often had to borrow money from people.

ⓒ He cut off part of his nose.

3 About how many paintings did Vincent van Gogh make in his life?

ⓐ 900

ⓑ 1,890

ⓒ 2,000

4 Which painting did Vincent van Gogh NOT paint?

ⓐ *The Potato Eaters*

ⓑ *Impression: Sunrise*

ⓒ *Starry Night*

5 Fill in the blank with the correct word(s).

Vincent van Gogh sold one painting during his lifetime, but his paintings are worth ____________________ today.

Vocabulary

Match the words and phrases with their definitions.

6	commercial	ⓐ education one receives at a school
7	formal training	ⓑ madness; insanity; a sickness of the brain
8	mental illness	ⓒ relating to business
9	commit suicide	ⓓ known to people
10	recognizable	ⓔ to kill oneself

Listening Skills Practice: Note-Taking II

What is note-taking?

Note-taking is a way to organize and write down important information in a talk. Do not write sentences when you take notes. That takes too much time. Instead, focus on the key words and phrases the speaker says. Do not write words like *a*, *an*, and *the*. Do not write verbs like *am*, *is*, and *are* either. Just write the important words and phrases.

A Circle the important words and phrases in each sentence.

ⓐ This caused him to cut off part of his ear and to commit suicide when he was thirty-seven years old.

ⓑ He created more than 2,000 works of art in his life. Around 900 of them were paintings.

ⓒ But van Gogh's style changed later in his life. He began painting with vibrant bright colors.

B Listen to a talk by an art gallery guide related to the topic and answer the questions.

Memo

1 Where is the Vincent van Gogh Museum?

ⓐ Paris

ⓑ London

ⓒ Amsterdam

2 Which statement about the Vincent van Gogh Museum is true?

ⓐ A private collector owns the museum.

ⓑ It has more than 200 works by Vincent van Gogh.

ⓒ It is on the site of Vincent van Gogh's family home.

3 Listen to the talk again. Take notes on the following topics.

ⓐ Vincent van Gogh Museum location: ______________________

ⓑ Vincent van Gogh Museum permanent exhibit: ______________________

ⓒ Vincent van Gogh Museum types of paintings: ______________________

Chapter

5

The Environment

Unit 17

Pollution

Pre-Listening Questions

Answer the following questions.

1 What can you see in each picture?

2 What is pollution?

3 What causes pollution?

4 How can we prevent pollution?

Vocabulary

Write the correct word or phrase from the box for each definition.

waterway	fertilizer	manmade	soil	pollute	landfill

1 ____________ to make something dirty

2 ____________ a garbage dump; a large area where people take their trash

3 ____________ earth; ground

4 ____________ a river or other type of passage that ships use to travel on

5 ____________ not natural; made by a person

6 ____________ a type of chemical that helps plants grow better

Pollution

Listen to the talk. Fill in the blanks as you listen.

When a person ______________ to the environment, that individual is ______________. There are several kinds of pollution. But there are ______________. They are ______________.

Air pollution affects ______________. Most air pollution is manmade. It comes from many sources. The two major sources of pollution are ______________. Factories often ______________ the air. So do vehicles like ______________. Factories and vehicles create a lot of air pollution since they ______________. These are sources of energy such as ______________. Oil and coal are quite dirty, so ______________ a great deal of air pollution.

Water pollution is ______________ in many places, too. Water pollution ______________. As a result, people and animals can't drink the water. In addition, fish, other animals, and even plants can't ______________. Sadly, humans cause a lot of water pollution. Some people ______________ and chemicals into water sources. Other times, ______________ gets into waterways. ______________ can create water pollution, too. All of these things greatly harm the Earth's ______________.

The third major type is ______________. This happens when ______________. Once again, ______________ very much soil pollution. Farmers can pollute the soil by using insecticide ______________. Miners can harm the ground ______________ in certain ways. And ______________, where people take their garbage, can cause a large amount of soil pollution.

Organizer Listen to the talk again. Then, fill in the blanks with the correct words.

Pollution

- Air pollution
  - Two major sources are factories and ⓐ __________
  - Burn dirty ⓑ __________ such as coal and oil
- ⓒ __________ pollution
  - Makes clean water dirty
  - Can't drink, and animals and plants can't live in it
  - Is caused by garbage, chemicals, and ⓓ __________
- Soil pollution
  - Happens when the ground gets pollution
  - Can be caused by farmers and ⓔ __________
  - Is caused by ⓕ __________

Main Topic

Circle the correct answer.

1 What is the main topic of the talk?

ⓐ Three different types of pollution

ⓑ How most pollution is caused

ⓒ The best way to get rid of pollution

Details

Answer the questions.

2 What is NOT responsible for a lot of air pollution?

ⓐ Vehicles

ⓑ Factories

ⓒ Ships

3 How do some humans cause water pollution?

ⓐ They sail boats on lakes.

ⓑ They dump chemicals into waterways.

ⓒ They go fishing in oceans.

4 Who often causes soil pollution?

ⓐ Miners

ⓑ Drivers

ⓒ Sailors

5 Fill in the blank with the correct word(s).

Pollution happens when a person adds something ________________ to the environment.

Vocabulary

Match the words and phrases with their definitions.

6 breathe •	• ⓐ to take air into the body and then to push it out
7 insecticide •	• ⓑ dangerous
8 water source •	• ⓒ a poison used to kill insects
9 harmful •	• ⓓ to throw away; to put in the trash
10 dump •	• ⓔ a place such as an ocean, lake, or river that contains a large amount of water

Listening Skills Practice: Classification I

What is classification?

Classification involves putting people, places, or things into groups. Many talks contain information about two or more groups. These groups may have their own characteristics. Listen carefully to the talk. Then, put each of the characteristics into the correct group. By using classification, you can understand the differences between these groups.

A Listen to the talk again. Then, complete the classification charts.

Air Pollution	Water Pollution	Soil Pollution
- Is mostly manmade	- Makes clean water dirty	- Happens when ⓔ ___________ gets polluted
- Major sources are ⓐ ___________	- People and animals can't drink water	- Caused by ⓕ ___________
- Release harmful chemicals	- Caused by ⓒ ___________ and chemicals	- Can be caused by landfills
- Burn ⓑ ___________	- Caused by fertilizer and ⓓ ___________	

B Listen to another talk related to the topic and answer the questions.

NOTE

1 Why are electric cars good for the environment?

ⓐ They can transport many people at the same time.

ⓑ They do not burn any gasoline.

ⓒ They can only run for a short amount of time.

2 What should farmers use less of in their fields?

ⓐ Fertilizer

ⓑ Insecticide

ⓒ Seeds

3 Complete the classification chart about how to improve the environment.

How to Improve the Environment

- Use ⓐ ___________ less often
- Take buses, subways, and other forms of ⓑ ___________
- Buy ⓒ ___________
- Farmers can use ⓓ ___________ in their fields
- Reduce ⓔ ___________ in the ocean

Unit
18 Natural Resources

Pre-Listening Questions

Answer the following questions.

1 What can you see in each picture?

2 What are natural resources?

3 Why are they important to us?

4 Should we conserve our natural resources? Why or why not?

Vocabulary

Write the correct word or phrase from the box for each definition.

replace	abundant	biotic	abiotic	category	conserve

1 ____________ alive; living

2 ____________ plentiful; existing in great amount or number

3 ____________ to save; to preserve

4 ____________ not alive; not living

5 ____________ to substitute one thing for another

6 ____________ a group; a class

Natural Resources

Listen to the talk. Fill in the blanks as you listen.

Anything that is not manmade is ________________. There are all kinds of them. Some are living. Those are ________________. Others are ________________. Those are abiotic resources. Biotic resources include ________________ such as cows and sheep, wild animals, and fish. A few abiotic resources are ________________. Some natural resources are ________________. Others aren't valuable at all.

There are ________________ natural resources on the Earth. So, while there's ________________, there are ________________. In addition, there are ________________ of natural resources: renewable resources and ________________.

Renewable resources can ________________. Or they ________________. For instance, there's ________________ sunlight. Air, wind, and water are also abundant. Thus people can use them ________________. Trees, fruits, and vegetables are ________________. People can grow them fairly quickly. Animals are renewable resources, too. For example, cows, sheep, chickens, pigs, and ________________.

On the other hand, nonrenewable resources ________________. Coal, oil, and gas are fossil fuels. They ________________ that people use. Yet there are limited supplies of all three. It ________________ for them to be produced. ________________ to make energy, they cannot be used again. ________________, and other metals are also nonrenewable resources. There are ________________ of all of them. Thus people need to conserve them so that they don't run out.

Organizer Listen to the talk again. Then, fill in the blanks with the correct words.

Renewable Resources

- Can be easily replaced or never ⓐ ____________
- Are ⓑ ____________, air, wind, and water
- Are animals since they ⓒ ____________
- Include trees, fruits, and vegetables

Nonrenewable Resources

- Are limited ⓓ ____________
- Are ⓔ ____________ such as coal, oil, and gas
- Must ⓕ ____________ so that they don't run out
- Include gold, silver, iron, and other metals

Comprehension

Main Topic

Circle the correct answer.

1 What is the main idea of the talk?

ⓐ There are both renewable and nonrenewable natural resources.

ⓑ People need to conserve all of the Earth's natural resources.

ⓒ Some natural resources are more important than others are.

Details

Answer the questions.

2 Which of the following is an abiotic natural resource?

ⓐ Sunlight

ⓑ Trees

ⓒ Cows

3 Which statement about renewable resources is NOT true?

ⓐ They include all kinds of animals.

ⓑ Some of them never run out.

ⓒ They can be very hard to find.

4 What are nonrenewable resources?

ⓐ Resources that come from the ground

ⓑ Resources that are limited in supply

ⓒ Resources that are alive

5 Fill in the blank with the correct word(s).

________________ resources include fossil fuels and metals such as gold, silver, and iron.

Vocabulary

Match the words and phrases with their definitions.

6 rare metal •	• ⓐ main; major
7 reproduce •	• ⓑ a metal such as gold or silver that is uncommon
8 primary •	• ⓒ to make babies; to create young animals
9 endless •	• ⓓ a limited amount of something
10 finite supply •	• ⓔ not ending; forever

Listening Skills Practice: Classification II

What is classification?

Classification involves putting information about people, places, or things into different groups. People, places, and things often have different features. Listen carefully to the talk. Then, put each feature into the correct group. By using classification, you can understand how the groups are similar to and different from each other.

A Listen to the talk again. Then, complete the classification charts.

Renewable Resources

- Can be replaced easily or ⓐ ___________
- Are big supplies of sunlight, ⓑ ___________
- Are trees, ⓒ ___________
- Are animals such as cows, sheep, chickens, and pigs

Nonrenewable Resources

- Are ⓓ ___________ in supply
- Are fossil fuels such as ⓔ ___________
- Cannot be used again
- Are gold, ⓕ ___________, and other metals
- People need to conserve them

B Listen to a news broadcast related to the topic and answer the questions.

Memo

1 What have many environmentalists claimed?

ⓐ People need to look harder for oil.

ⓑ The Earth's oil supply will be gone soon.

ⓒ It should be illegal to search for oil.

2 Where are there many shale oil fields?

ⓐ England

ⓑ Spain

ⓒ Canada

3 Complete the classification chart about the Earth's increasing oil supply.

The Earth's Increasing Oil Supply

- Are improvements in ⓐ ___________
- Know there are oil fields beneath ⓑ ___________
- Are ⓒ ___________ fields
- Are oil ⓓ ___________
- Can ⓔ ___________ both places nowadays

Unit 19

Recycling

Pre-Listening Questions

Answer the following questions.

1 What are the people in the picture holding?

2 What is recycling?

3 What kinds of objects can people recycle?

4 How do you feel about recycling? Why do you feel that way?

Vocabulary

Write the correct word or phrase from the box for each definition.

merely	overflowing	limited	sort	reuse	preserve

1 ____________ simply; just; only

2 ____________ to use again

3 ____________ to keep; to save

4 ____________ restricted in amount

5 ____________ spilling over; so great that something cannot be held by its container

6 ____________ to arrange by type

Recycling

Listen to the talk. Fill in the blanks as you listen.

These days, most people __________ all of their trash into one bag and then throw it away. They __________. Thus they don't __________. Instead, they __________ so that they can be recycled. Recycling is a great way __________. There are many items people can recycle. Paper, plastic, glass, and metal products __________. It's __________ and textiles, too.

There are __________. First of all, it allows people to preserve __________. This is especially true of __________. The amount of metals in the ground is limited. By recycling products __________, people can reduce the amount of metals that __________ from the ground. Likewise, by recycling paper, people will be able to __________.

Another benefit of recycling is that people will __________ if they recycle. Landfills are enormous places where people __________. Unfortunately, lots of these landfills are overflowing. There's __________ in them. By recycling, people can __________ that's taken to landfills. As a result, landfills will __________.

By recycling, people can also reduce the amount of pollution __________. For instance, __________ have chemicals in them. These __________ the ground. But, if people recycle them, then these items __________. Thus, by recycling, people can make sure that the Earth is __________.

Organizer Listen to the talk again. Then, fill in the blanks with the correct words.

Recycling

- Is a way to ⓐ __________ various products
- Can recycle paper, plastic, glass, and ⓑ __________
- Can recycle electronics and ⓒ __________
- Lets people preserve ⓓ __________ natural resources
- Can produce ⓔ __________
- Can reduce ⓕ __________ pollution

Comprehension

Main Topic

Circle the correct answer.

1 What is the main idea of the talk?

ⓐ Some items can cause various types of pollution.

ⓑ There are many benefits to recycling various items.

ⓒ Everyone should be sure to recycle certain items.

Details

Answer the questions.

2 Which of the following statements is NOT true?

ⓐ There are only two benefits to recycling.

ⓑ It is possible to recycle electronic items.

ⓒ People sort their garbage to recycle items.

3 Which type of product is limited in amount?

ⓐ Water

ⓑ Metals

ⓒ Air

4 How can recycling help landfills?

ⓐ It can reduce the amount of air pollution in them.

ⓑ It can help landfills earn more money.

ⓒ It can make them fill up more slowly.

5 Fill in the blank with the correct word(s).

Many items, such as __________________, metal, paper, and plastic products, can be recycled.

Vocabulary

Match the words and phrases with their definitions.

6	set aside	• •	ⓐ to throw away
7	dispose of	• •	ⓑ a product made from cloth
8	textile	• •	ⓒ to remove something of value from the ground
9	mine	• •	ⓓ to save; to put away somewhere else
10	precious	• •	ⓔ valuable

Listening Skills Practice: Understanding Organization I

What is understanding organization?

Understanding organization lets people understand why speakers provide certain information in their talks. Speakers include facts for various reasons. For example, they may mention facts to make comparisons, to provide extra information, and to give examples. Listen carefully to understand why the speakers mention certain things in their talks.

A Listen to the talk again. Then, answer the following questions.

ⓐ Why does the speaker mention electronics and textiles?

ⓘ To say that people can recycle them

ⓘⓘ To compare them with glass and metal products

ⓑ Why does the speaker discuss landfills?

ⓘ To explain how they can benefit from recycling

ⓘⓘ To complain that there are not enough of them

B Listen to another talk related to the topic and answer the questions.

NOTE

1 What is on the Recycling Loop?

ⓐ Three green arrows

ⓑ Three words

ⓒ Three recycling bins

2 Why does the speaker mention newspapers, plastic bottles, aluminum cans, and glassware?

ⓐ To compare and contrast them with each other

ⓑ To claim that they are valuable items

ⓒ To name some items that people can recycle

3 Why does the speaker describe the processing stage?

ⓐ To show what happens during that stage

ⓑ To explain why she dislikes recycling

ⓒ To prove it is more important than the buying stage

Unit 20

Renewable Energy

Pre-Listening Questions

Answer the following questions.

1 What can you see in each picture?

2 What is renewable energy?

3 What can people use to produce renewable energy?

4 What are some advantages of renewable energy? What are some disadvantages of it?

Vocabulary

Write the correct word or phrase from the box for each definition.

blade	inefficient	practical	maintenance	fragile	volcanic

1 ____________ relating to volcanoes

2 ____________ delicate; easily broken

3 ____________ wasteful; ineffective

4 ____________ work done to keep equipment running well

5 ____________ a sharp object such as a knife or sword

6 ____________ useful

Renewable Energy

Listen to the talk. Fill in the blanks as you listen.

Around the world, fossil fuels ____________________ of people's energy needs. The main ones are coal, oil, and gas. They are very ____________________. But there is a limited supply of them. Thus they are ____________________. The fossil fuel supply will run out in the future. So people are looking for new energy sources. Many are turning ____________________.

Renewable energy can be used ____________________. The supply of it ____________________. There are ____________________. They include solar power, hydroelectric power, ____________________, and geothermal power.

Solar power ____________________. Hydroelectric power comes from ____________________. Wind power uses the wind ____________________. Tidal power uses ____________________ to make energy. And geothermal power uses the heat from ____________________ to make energy.

There are ____________________ to renewable energy. First, it won't run out. Second, it's ____________________. It creates ____________________. Third, the facilities that create electricity often ____________________. So they're ____________________.

There are ____________________ though. For instance, they ____________________ everywhere. Solar energy isn't ____________________. Geothermal energy can only be used in regions ____________________. At the present time, they are ____________________, too. Finally, they can have negative effects on their regions. Many ____________________ lots of birds with their blades. And dams over rivers can ____________________.

Organizer Listen to the talk again. Then, fill in the blanks with the correct words.

Renewable Energy

- Is ⓐ __________ from nonrenewable energy such as fossil fuels
- Can be used again and again
- Includes solar, ⓑ __________, wind, tidal, and geothermal power

- Will not ⓒ __________
- Is ⓓ __________ so produces little or no pollution
- Cannot be used ⓔ __________ though
- Is inefficient and expensive and can have ⓕ __________ effects in some places

Comprehension

Main Topic

Circle the correct answer.

1 What is the main topic of the talk?

ⓐ How nonrenewable and renewable energy are different

ⓑ The most popular types of renewable energy

ⓒ The types of renewable energy and their advantages

Details

Answer the questions.

2 Where does geothermal energy come from?

ⓐ Heat inside the Earth

ⓑ The heat of the sun

ⓒ Ocean tides

3 Which is NOT an advantage of renewable energy?

ⓐ It can be used anywhere.

ⓑ It will never run out.

ⓒ It creates little pollution.

4 What is a negative effect of wind turbines?

ⓐ They only work at certain times.

ⓑ They kill lots of birds with their blades.

ⓒ They are extremely noisy.

5 Fill in the blank with the correct word(s).

People are turning to renewable energy because the Earth's supply of ________________ will run out someday.

Vocabulary

Match the words and phrases with their definitions.

6	efficient	ⓐ to use; to resort to
7	wind turbine	ⓑ capable; working well
8	turn to	ⓒ a type of fuel such as coal, gas, or oil
9	ocean tide	ⓓ a windmill; an object that can make energy from the wind
10	fossil fuel	ⓔ the rising and falling of the level of the ocean at shore

Listening Skills Practice: Understanding Organization II

What is understanding organization?

Understanding organization lets people understand why speakers provide certain information in their talks. Speakers include facts for various reasons. For example, they may mention facts to give detailed explanations, to provide causes and effects, and to put information into groups. Listen carefully to understand why the speakers mention certain things in their talks.

A **Listen to the talk again. Then, answer the following questions.**

ⓐ Why does the speaker mention coil, oil, and gas?
- ⓘ To explain how they can make energy
- ⓘⓘ To name them as types of fossil fuels

ⓑ Why does the speaker discuss the disadvantages of renewable energy?
- ⓘ To show that they have some drawbacks
- ⓘⓘ To describe how to solve these problems

B **Listen to a talk by a hydroelectric power plant employee related to the topic and answer the questions.**

Memo

1 What kind of power plant is at the dam?
- ⓐ A geothermal one
- ⓑ A hydroelectric one
- ⓒ A coal-fired one

2 Why does the speaker mention cheap electricity?
- ⓐ To say that the coal-fired plant provides it
- ⓑ To promise it in the near future
- ⓒ To state that it is a benefit of the dam

3 Why does the speaker discuss fish ladders?
- ⓐ To explain how salmon get past the dam
- ⓑ To state when they will be installed
- ⓒ To show the listeners where they are located

Answers

Answers

Chapter 1 Natural Disasters

Unit 01 Krakatoa

p. 11

Pre-Listening Questions Sample Answer

1 It was a volcano.
2 It erupted a long time ago. I think the eruption was very powerful.
3 It often shoots out lava. Rocks, gas, and ash may come out, too.
4 There are some volcanoes in my country. Halla Mountain and Baekdu Mountain are two of them. But they don't erupt anymore.

Vocabulary

1	eruption	2	lava
3	expel	4	sunset
5	sunrise	6	tsunami

p. 12

Script

M Teacher: There are all kinds of natural disasters. Hurricanes, typhoons, and tornadoes are three of them. Earthquakes are another. Volcanoes can cause them, too. When volcanoes erupt, they can be highly destructive. They often spew ash, poisonous gas, rocks, and lava. They can injure and kill many people. They can even affect the environment.

On August 26, 1883, the volcano Krakatoa erupted. It was one of the strongest eruptions in modern times. Krakatoa was located in Indonesia. It was on the island of Rakata. In 1883, it hadn't erupted for more than 200 years. It had been dormant for very long, so people weren't afraid of it. But, on the morning of August 26, it erupted. In fact, it erupted four times that morning. The volcano expelled a cloud of ash. It rose more than twenty-five kilometers into the sky. Krakatoa also spewed hot rocks that landed as far as forty kilometers away. And the eruption destroyed the island of Rakata.

Because the eruption was so loud, people in faraway places could hear it. In fact, people more than 4,500 kilometers away heard it. The eruption caused numerous tsunamis to form. They destroyed many villages on nearby Indonesian islands. In total, more than 36,000 people died.

Krakatoa didn't just have a local effect though. Since it was such a strong eruption, it had a global effect. It threw a great amount of dust in the air. After the eruption, sunrises in some places looked green. And sunsets around the world looked red due to all of the dust. The following year, the weather around the world became much cooler. Temperatures around the world didn't return to normal until five years after the eruption.

Organizer

ⓐ dormant	ⓑ hot rocks
ⓒ tsunamis	ⓓ global
ⓔ red	ⓕ Weather

p. 13

Comprehension

1	ⓑ	2	ⓑ	3	ⓒ
4	ⓐ	5	strongest		
6	ⓓ	7	ⓐ	8	ⓑ
9	ⓒ	10	ⓔ		

p. 14

Listening Skills Practice: Cause and Effect I

A ⓐ ⓘⓘⓘ ⓑ ⓘⓘ ⓒ ⓘ

B

Script

W Teacher: The volcano Krakatoa erupted in 1883. It was one of the most powerful eruptions in history. In fact, many experts believe that it was the fifth most powerful eruption. It was so strong that the volcano destroyed the island it was located on. It caused a lot of damage to the islands around it, too. The island was gone for many years. But, in 1927, a new island began to rise from the sea. It was named Anak Krakatoa. It means "Child of Krakatoa." The island is volcanic. There have been several minor eruptions since 1927. Because of them, the volcano has been rising higher and higher. Today, Anak Krakatoa is around 300 meters high. It's an active volcano. Scientists believe that it could erupt as powerfully as it did in 1883 in the future. This would be a disaster. Nowadays, many people live near it, so a powerful eruption could kill more than 100,000 people. Because a big eruption could cause tsunamis, even more people could die, too.

1 ⓑ
2 ⓐ
3 ⓐ so ⓑ Because ⓒ because

Unit 02 The San Francisco Earthquake

p. 15

Pre-Listening Questions Sample Answer

1 I see a lot of buildings that have been destroyed.
2 Maybe there was an earthquake.
3 An earthquake happens when the ground starts to shake.
4 No, I haven't. I don't want to be in an earthquake. I heard they are very scary.

Vocabulary

1	population	2	destruction
3	measure	4	suffer
5	aftershock	6	coast

p. 16

Script

W Teacher: San Francisco is a city in the northern part of California. In 1906, it was the largest city on the American west coast. It was also the ninth biggest city in the country. More than 400,000 people lived in San Francisco. In addition to being a big city, it was also an important one in the United States.

Then, at 5:12 AM on April 18, 1906, disaster struck. A powerful earthquake hit the city. An earthquake happens when the ground begins to move. This earthquake was very strong. It lasted for nearly one minute. People as far away as Los Angeles were able to feel the earthquake. It measured between 7.7 and 7.9 on the Richter scale.

Since the earthquake was so strong, it caused a great deal of damage. A large number of buildings were destroyed. There were also powerful aftershocks. These are weaker earthquakes that come after a big tremor. They caused even more damage to the city.

However, the earthquake didn't cause the greatest amount of damage. Instead, a fire caused the most destruction. The earthquake damaged some gas lines in San Francisco. So many small fires started from these damaged lines. Then, a huge fire began. It lasted for four days. By the time it ended, it had affected a huge part of the city.

Around 3,000 people probably died because of the earthquake and fire. In addition, more than 200,000 people became homeless after these two disasters. That was half of the city's population. The city suffered hundreds of millions of dollars in damage. The San Francisco Earthquake was one of the worst natural disasters ever to affect the United States.

Organizer

ⓐ 1906	ⓑ one
ⓒ aftershocks	ⓓ damage
ⓔ gas lines	ⓕ died

p. 17

Comprehension

1	ⓐ	2	ⓒ	3	ⓒ
4	ⓑ	5	fire		
6	ⓔ	7	ⓓ	8	ⓒ
9	ⓐ	10	ⓑ		

p. 18

Listening Skills Practice: Cause and Effect II

A ⓐ ⅲ ⓑ ⅰ ⓒ ⅱ

B

Script

W Student: For my report, I want to talk about the New Madrid Earthquake. The New Madrid Earthquake happened on February 7, 1812. There were actually three strong earthquakes in the same area before it took place. But the earthquake on February 7 was the strongest. In fact, it was the strongest earthquake ever recorded on the continental United States. Geologists believe that it was at least 8.0 on the Richter scale.

New Madrid is a place in the state of Missouri. Most people don't imagine earthquakes happening there. But because there is a fault in the Earth's crust in that area, sometimes strong tremors take place. The February 7 earthquake caused the ground to change shape. Some areas sank. New lakes formed in some places. It was so strong that the Mississippi River started to flow north. The river usually flows south. Fortunately, few people lived in the area then. So only a small number of people were killed or injured.

1 ⓑ
2 ⓑ
3 ⓐ Because ⓑ so ⓒ because

Unit 03 The Tunguska Event

p. 19

Pre-Listening Questions Sample Answer

1 Something destroyed all of the trees. Maybe there was a big fire.
2 I'm not sure. Some of them are small, but others are many kilometers in diameter.
3 It can destroy a big area and kill many people. If it hits the ocean, it can cause a tsunami to form.
4 Millions of years ago, an asteroid hit the Earth and killed all of the dinosaurs.

Vocabulary

1 latter	2 explode
3 rare	4 diameter
5 estimate	6 speck

p. 20

Script

M Teacher: Every day, thousands of meteors enter the Earth's atmosphere. Most are tiny specks of dust. Others are no larger than a grain of rice. At times, rocks the size of a baseball or basketball enter the Earth's atmosphere. Most of these meteors burn up in the air. Those are the streaks of light we see in the night sky. On rare occasions, large meteors not only enter the Earth's atmosphere, but they also don't burn up. They may hit the ground. Or they may explode near the ground. The latter happened in Tunguska, Russia, many years ago.

Tunguska is a remote area in Siberia, Russia. Most people around the world had never heard of it. That changed on June 30, 1908, though. On that morning, a large meteor entered the Earth's atmosphere. Astronomers estimate that it was between fifty and 200 meters in diameter. It probably weighed more than one hundred million kilograms. And it was moving around 20,000 kilometers per hour.

Between five and ten kilometers above the Earth's surface, the meteor exploded. The explosion was 1,000 times more powerful than the atomic bomb dropped on Hiroshima, Japan, during World War II. Fortunately, the meteor exploded in a forested area with few people. The explosion destroyed most of the trees in a region covering more than 2,000 square kilometers. When the meteor blew up, it became brighter than the sun.

This became known as the Tunguska Event. It showed people how dangerous meteors can be. If the meteor had hit a populated region, millions of people would have died. So now many astronomers spend time looking for dangerous meteors in space.

Organizer

ⓐ Thousands	ⓑ hit
ⓒ streaks	ⓓ Russia
ⓔ trees	ⓕ 1,000

p. 21

Comprehension

1 ⓑ	2 ⓒ	3 ⓐ
4 ⓑ	5 large	
6 ⓔ	7 ⓐ	8 ⓒ
9 ⓑ	10 ⓓ	

p. 22

Listening Skills Practice: Connecting Words I

A ⓐ But ⓑ When ⓒ And

B

Script

M Teacher: For millions of years, dinosaurs were the dominant animals on the planet. Then, about sixty-five million years ago, they disappeared. The dinosaurs died, and the age of mammals began. For the longest time, scientists didn't know what had killed the dinosaurs. Now, they believe that they know the answer: It was an enormous asteroid.

In the Yucatan Peninsula in Mexico, there's a huge crater. It's about 180 kilometers in diameter. It's likely that an asteroid more than ten kilometers wide created it. Scientists have dated this crater to sixty-five million years ago. They believe the asteroid hit the Earth and killed the dinosaurs. When it hit the ground, it threw a great deal of dust into the air. This kept the sun from shining on most of the planet. As a result, global temperatures dropped. This killed most of the plant life on the Earth. Thus many animals had no food to eat. The dinosaurs also couldn't handle the cold temperatures. So they died and went extinct.

1 ⓒ
2 ⓒ
3 ⓐ Then ⓑ so ⓒ when

Unit 04 The Southeast Asian Tsunami

p. 23

Pre-Listening Questions Sample Answer

1 There's a huge wave. It's about to hit the land.
2 I guess a big wave hit that area.
3 It's a large wave that moves quickly and hits the land.
4 A huge earthquake caused it. And it killed many people in different countries.

Vocabulary

1	village	2	donate
3	inland	4	destructive
5	recede	6	suffer

p. 24

Script

W Teacher: Earthquakes don't just happen on land. They frequently happen underwater. When there's a big underwater earthquake, it can affect the water on the surface. An underwater tremor can create a tsunami. A tsunami can be incredibly destructive. It starts as a very fast-moving wave of water. But, as it approaches shore, something unique happens. The water near shore recedes away from the coast. It can go back hundreds of meters. Then, as the tsunami gets closer to land, it slows down. The water that recedes becomes a part of the tsunami. This increases the size of the wave. So a huge wave of water may hit land. Some tsunamis can be several meters high. They can also go far inland.

On December 26, 2004, there was a major tsunami. In the morning, a powerful underwater earthquake took place in the Indian Ocean. It measured 9.0 on the Richter scale. It created a large number of tsunamis all over the Indian Ocean. At least eighteen countries in the region were hit by tsunamis. Some were fairly minor. Others were enormous.

Many towns, villages, and cities along the coast were wiped out. More than 230,000 people lost their lives. At least one million people lost their homes. Indonesia suffered the most. More than 160,000 people died there. Thousands of people also died in Thailand, Sri Lanka, and India. In addition, thousands of people went missing and have never been seen or heard from again.

Thankfully, people around the world donated billions of dollars in aid after the tsunami. The recovery was difficult in many countries. But the aid money helped the survivors try to get their lives back together.

Organizer

ⓐ underwater	ⓑ fast-moving
ⓒ size	ⓓ recedes
ⓔ 2004	ⓕ homes

p. 25

Comprehension

1	ⓐ	2	ⓐ	3	ⓒ
4	ⓑ	5	million		
6	ⓑ	7	ⓐ	8	ⓓ
9	ⓒ	10	ⓔ		

p. 26

Listening Skills Practice: Connecting Words II

A ⓐ as ⓑ and ⓒ so

B

Script

M News Broadcaster: Yesterday, March 11, 2011, there was an underwater earthquake in Japan. It was about 270 kilometers northeast of Tokyo. The earthquake registered 9.0 on the Richter scale. It was one of the strongest earthquakes in history. As a result, there were a number of tsunamis. They hit the east coast of Japan. According to reports, some of them were around ten meters high.

Many coastal towns and villages have suffered a lot of damage. It's feared that thousands of people may have died. Japanese news reports say that huge numbers of homes and buildings have been destroyed. There are also fires raging in many places. Another problem is that the tsunamis hit several nuclear reactors. Officials are very worried about a nuclear reactor in Fukushima. It suffered a loss of power. And its backup generators are not working either. Hopefully, that won't develop into a major problem. We'll try to learn more as quickly as we can.

1 ⓑ
2 ⓐ
3 ⓐ so ⓑ and ⓒ and

Chapter 2 **Fantasy Worlds**

Unit 05 Narnia

p. 29

Pre-Listening Questions Sample Answer

1 They are *The Lion, the Witch, and the Wardrobe*, *Prince Caspian*, *The Voyage of the Dawn Treader*, *The Silver Chair*, *The Horse and His Boy*, *The Magician's Nephew*, and *The Last Battle*.

2 It's a magical land. There are many talking animals there.

3 I think it would be great. I would love to talk to my dog and other animals.

4 Middle-earth is the fantasy world from *The Lord of the Rings*.

Vocabulary

1 somehow
2 feature
3 dryad
4 wardrobe
5 witch
6 faun

p. 30

Script

M Teacher: One day, four children are playing in big house. The children's names are Peter, Susan, Edmund, and Lucy. They open the door to a wardrobe and discover another world inside it. The name of this world is Narnia. It's a fantasy world much different from ours. For example, many of the animals in Narnia can speak. There are talking beavers, dogs, birds, and other animals. Numerous creatures from mythology live there, too. There are fauns, centaurs, and dryads as well as all kinds of horrible monsters.

The children find out that Narnia is in the middle of a 100-year-long winter. The White Witch has created this terrible winter. She is the evil ruler of Narnia. Fortunately, Aslan is in Narnia. He is the great lion, the son of the Emperor-Over-The-Sea, and the true king of Narnia. The children then meet Aslan, fight the White Witch, and defeat her army. After that, they become the kings and queens of Narnia.

This is the story of *The Lion, the Witch, and the Wardrobe*. It was written by British author C.S. Lewis. *The Lion, the Witch, and the Wardrobe* is the first book of *The Chronicles of Narnia*. It is also the most popular of the books about Narnia. There are seven books in the series. All seven of the books feature children from our world who somehow get transported to Narnia. There, they have all kinds of wonderful adventures.

The Chronicles of Narnia are some of the most beloved children's books in the world. They have sold millions of copies. Some movies based on the books have become very popular as well.

Organizer

ⓐ fantasy
ⓑ Aslan
ⓒ White Witch
ⓓ seven
ⓔ Narnia
ⓕ *the Wardrobe*

p. 31

Comprehension

1 ⓑ
2 ⓒ
3 ⓒ
4 ⓒ
5 talking
6 ⓓ
7 ⓔ
8 ⓐ
9 ⓒ
10 ⓑ

p. 32

Listening Skills Practice: Details I

A ⓐ wardrobe, Narnia
ⓑ Aslan, kings and queens
ⓒ seven, *The Lion, the Witch, and the Wardrobe*

B

Script

M Teacher: C.S. Lewis created several memorable characters in his Narnia books. Two are Mr. Tumnus and Reepicheep. Mr. Tumnus is a faun. A faun is a mythological creature that's half man and half goat. In *The Lion, the Witch, and the Wardrobe*, Lucy enters Narnia before the other children, and she meets Mr. Tumnus. At first, Mr. Tumnus plans to tell the White Witch about Lucy. But he and Lucy become good friends instead. The White Witch turns Mr. Tumnus into a statue. Yet Aslan restores him to life later in the book. As for Reepicheep, he's the leader of the talking mice in Narnia. He appears in three of the seven Narnia books. He appears in *Prince Caspian*, *The Voyage of the Dawn Treader*, and *The Last Battle*. Although he is small, Reepicheep is extremely brave. He is also always willing to fight. He is very concerned about honor, so he treats people in a polite manner. He is often involved in many comedic scenes as well.

1 ⓒ

2 ⓐ

3 ⓐ T ⓑ F ⓒ T

Unit 06 Middle-Earth

p. 33

Pre-Listening Questions Sample Answer

1 I can see a gold ring and a home in a hill.

2 I read all three books in the trilogy and loved them. I also loved all of the movies.

3 It's a frightening fantasy land. There are all kinds of dangerous monsters and evil creatures living in it.

4 Elves, dwarves, hobbits, ents, and orcs all live in Middle-earth.

Vocabulary

1	decade	2	quest
3	awful	4	fearsome
5	trilogy	6	elf

p. 34

Script

W Teacher: As a young boy, J.R.R. Tolkien studied languages, literature, and mythology. The knowledge he gained from his studies later helped him create the fantasy world Middle-earth.

Tolkien wrote about Middle-earth over a period of decades. It is a land with many races of creatures. There are humans. Elves and dwarves live there, too. The elves live in the forests while the dwarves live in caves underground. There are tree creatures called Ents as well as awful monsters such as orcs. Great and powerful wizards wander the land. Finally, there are hobbits. They are small humanlike creatures that lived in a part of Middle-earth called the Shire.

Tolkien wrote several books that were based in Middle-earth. One was called *The Silmarillion*. Tolkien wrote it first, but it was published after he died. It tells the story of the creation and early years of Middle Earth. In 1937, he published *The Hobbit*. This was his first published work based in Middle-earth. The book is about a hobbit named Bilbo Baggins. He, a group of dwarves, and the wizard Gandalf go on an adventure to kill a fearsome dragon.

The best-known books based in Middle-earth are the three books that make up *The Lord of the Rings* trilogy. They tell the story of the quest to destroy the One Ring. The books feature Gandalf and other wizards. There are hobbits, elves, dwarves, and men. There are enormous armies of evil men and monsters. The books tell an epic tale of good overcoming evil. They have been popular for decades, and it's likely that people will continue reading them far into the future.

Organizer

ⓐ dwarves	ⓑ orcs
ⓒ Shire	ⓓ creation
ⓔ dragon	ⓕ epic tale

p. 35

Comprehension

1	ⓒ	2	ⓐ	3	ⓑ
4	ⓐ	5	wizard		
6	ⓐ	7	ⓓ	8	ⓔ
9	ⓒ	10	ⓑ		

p. 36

Listening Skills Practice: Details II

A ⓐ elves, underground

ⓑ creation, died

ⓒ *The Lord of the Rings*, quest

B

Script

M Student: For my movie review, I will talk about *The Return of the King*. It's the third movie in *The Lord of the Rings* trilogy. The first two movies were *The Fellowship of the Ring* and *The Two Towers*. I thought this movie was excellent. In fact, it was one of the best movies I've ever seen. There are basically two stories in the movie. The first is the quest by Frodo Baggins and Samwise Gamgee to destroy the One Ring. They must go deep into the land of Mordor to do that. The second is about the great battles that take place between the forces of the evil Sauron and the armies of good. The battle scenes in the movie were amazing. When the movie ended, I wanted to see it again. I was also impressed that the events in the movie are similar to the ones the book. Many movies and books with the same titles are very different. But *The Return of the King* was not.

1 ⓒ

2 ⓑ

3 ⓐ F ⓑ T ⓒ F

Unit 07 The Magical World of Oz

p. 37

Pre-Listening Questions Sample Answer

1 Dorothy and her dog Toto are the main characters. There are also a scarecrow, a lion, and a tinman.

2 Oz is a magical land. There are witches and flying monkeys in it. There's a yellow brick road in it, too.

3 Yes, I have seen it before. I liked it a lot.

4 I have seen all of the *Harry Potter* movies, *The Lord of the Rings* movies, and *The Hobbit* movies.

Vocabulary

1 tiny 2 immediate

3 tornado 4 star

5 pleased 6 eventually

p. 38

Script

W Teacher: In 1939, a movie starring Judie Garland came out. At first, it wasn't very successful. Later, it was rereleased and became more popular. Then, in the 1950s, the film began airing on TV every year. Over time, it became one of the most loved movies in the world. The title of the movie was *The Wizard of Oz*.

The movie was based on the book *The Wonderful Wizard of Oz*. It was written by Frank Baum in 1900. In the story, Dorothy lives on a farm in Kansas. One day, there's a tornado. Dorothy and her dog Toto hide in the farmhouse, but the tornado picks up the house and carries it away. Eventually, the house lands in the magical land of Oz.

There are all kinds of strange creatures in Oz. First, Dorothy meets some tiny people called the Munchkins. She learns that her house fell on the Wicked Witch of the East and killed her. So the Munchkins are pleased to meet Dorothy. Dorothy, however, only wants to go home. She learns that she needs to visit the Emerald City. There, she can speak with the Wizard of Oz, who can help her.

On her way to the Emerald City, Dorothy makes friends with the Scarecrow, the Tin Woodman, and the Cowardly Lion. They have many adventures together in Oz. For instance, they have to deal with the Winged Monkeys as well as the Wicked Witch of the West. Eventually, Dorothy and Toto make it back to Kansas.

The Wonderful Wizard of Oz was an immediate hit. It was so popular that Baum wrote thirteen more books that took place in the fantasy land he had created.

Organizer

ⓐ 1900 ⓑ movie

ⓒ most loved ⓓ tornado

ⓔ Scarecrow ⓕ Eventually

p. 39

Comprehension

1 ⓐ 2 ⓒ 3 ⓐ

4 ⓑ 5 Emerald City

6 ⓔ 7 ⓑ 8 ⓐ

9 ⓒ 10 ⓓ

p. 40

Listening Skills Practice: Inference I

A ⓐ ⓘ ⓑ ⓘⓘ ⓒ ⓘⓘ

B

Script

M Teacher: In 1968, Ursula Le Guin published the book *A Wizard of Earthsea*. It was the first in a trilogy of books based in Earthsea. The other two books were *The Tombs of Atuan* and *The Farthest Shore*. Later, she published two more novels as well as several short stories that told about life in Earthsea. Earthsea is a land that's made up of islands. The people there live primitive lives. But Earthsea is also a magical land. Therefore wizards are common in some places. In addition, names have magic there. So telling a person one's true name can be dangerous. There are dragons in Earthsea as well. One of the main characters in the novels is Ged. *A Wizard of Earthsea* focuses on his early years as he trains to be a wizard and as he fights an evil being that he released into the world. The Earthsea books describe a detailed fantasy world that is loved by both young people and adults.

1 ⓒ 2 ⓐ 3 ⓒ

Unit 08 The World of *Harry Potter*

p. 41

Pre-Listening Questions Sample Answer

1 Harry Potter is a wizard. In the stories, people call him "the boy who lived."

2 I have read all of the books and seen all of the movies. Both are great, but I like the books more.

3 Ron Weasley and Hermione Granger are Harry's two best friends. Professor Dumbledore is the greatest wizard in the world. Lord Voldemort is the evil wizard. Hagrid and Professor Snape are two other characters.

4 It's a magical world, but wizards and witches use their magic in secret. Most non-magical people, called muggles, don't know that magic exists.

Vocabulary

1	imagine	2	enemy
3	wizard	4	ability
5	event	6	series

p. 42

Script

M Teacher: Imagine that some people in our world are different from everyone else. They aren't normal. Instead, they can use magic to do all sorts of things. Not only that, but there are also magical creatures such as dragons, elves, and goblins. There are magical items, too. And there's a war going on between good wizards and witches and evil ones as well. That's the world of *Harry Potter*.

Harry Potter is one of the most successful book and movie franchises ever. There are seven books in the series. They were written by J.K. Rowling. They've sold a combined total of more than 450 million copies. There are eight movies in the franchise. The movies have made nearly eight billion dollars in sales around the world.

The books and movies follow the lives of Harry Potter and his friends. The events in each book take around a year to occur. The first book is *Harry Potter and the Sorcerer's Stone*. In it, Harry finds out that he's a wizard. He begins taking classes at a school of magic called Hogwarts. He makes good friends such as Ron, Hermione, and Hagrid while he's at school. He also makes enemies such as Draco Malfoy.

In each book, Harry must battle the forces of the evil wizard Lord Voldemort. In some cases, he actually has to fight Voldemort, the most powerful wizard in the world, himself. Thanks to his own abilities as well as the skills of his friends, Harry manages to win these encounters. The battles aren't easy though, and sometimes his friends and family members die. In the last book, called *Harry Potter and the Deathly Hallows*, he has his final fight with Voldemort.

Organizer

ⓐ magical items	ⓑ seven
ⓒ lives	ⓓ Hogwarts
ⓔ evil	ⓕ Survives

p. 43

Comprehension

1	ⓑ	2	ⓑ	3	ⓐ
4	ⓑ	5	magical		
6	ⓓ	7	ⓔ	8	ⓒ
9	ⓐ	10	ⓑ		

p. 44

Listening Skills Practice: Inference II

A ⓐ ⓘⓘ ⓑ ⓘⓘ ⓒ ⓘ

B

Script

M Bookstore Employee: *Good afternoon, everyone.* Thanks for coming to the bookstore today. We've got a very special guest today. Our guest is Jim Butcher. He's the author of the highly successful fantasy series *The Dresden Files*. Just in case you don't know, let me tell you a little about the books. *The Dresden Files* focus on the life of Harry Dresden. He's a detective. But he's also a wizard. Harry lives in Chicago and solves cases that are related to magic. There are currently fifteen books in the series. Jim has plans to write a total of more than twenty books featuring Harry. At the beginning of the series, Harry is a fairly low-level wizard. However, as the books proceed, he gains more and more power. He also has to fight all sorts of bad guys. He has to deal with vampires, werewolves, trolls, fairies, evil wizards, and even strange beings called Outsiders. I highly recommend the Harry Dresden books. Now, let's hear from Jim.

1 ⓐ 2 ⓒ 3 ⓐ

Chapter 3 The Roman Era

Unit 09 Romulus and Remus

p. 47

Pre-Listening Questions Sample Answer

1 I can see two babies drinking the milk from a mother wolf.
2 I only know that it happened a long time ago.
3 Julius Caesar and Augustus Caesar were two famous people. The Emperor Nero is well-known, too.
4 The myths of Dangun and Hyukgeose are two of them. Hwanwoong, a god, married a woman who used to be a bear. They had a son, Dangun, who founded Gojoseon. Hyukgeose was the founding father of the Silla. He was born from an egg.

Vocabulary

1 riverbank 2 seize
3 argue 4 she-wolf
5 twins 6 shepherd

p. 48

Script

W Teacher: For nearly 1,000 years, Rome was among the most powerful cities in the world. It was the capital of both the Roman Republic and the Roman Empire. According to legend, it was founded in 753 B.C. The Romans had a myth about the founding of their city. It concerned the twins Romulus and Remus.

There was once a city in central Italy called Alba Longa. The king of Alba Longa was Numitor. He had a daughter named Rhea Silvia. One day, Numitor's brother Amulius seized the throne from Numitor. He killed Numitor's male children and sent Rhea away. Sometime later, Rhea became pregnant. She gave birth to twin boys. Their names were Romulus and Remus. And their father was Mars, the Roman god of war.

Amulius found out about Rhea's children. So he had them put in a basket. The basket was set in the Tiber River, and the twins floated off. However, the basket landed on the riverbank. There, a she-wolf found the twins. She protected them and let them drink her milk. A woodpecker got food for them. Later, some shepherds found the twins and raised them.

The twins eventually learned who their mother was. They worked together to kill Amulius. They put Numitor back onto the throne. They didn't want to wait to inherit the throne from their grandfather. So they decided to found their own city. They discovered a place by the Tiber River with seven hills. It was the perfect spot. But the twins argued over which hill they should build their city on. They got in a fight, and Romulus killed Remus. Romulus then built the city, which he called Rome.

Organizer

ⓐ throne ⓑ twins
ⓒ saved by ⓓ killed
ⓔ seven hills ⓕ 1,000

p. 49

Comprehension

1 ⓐ 2 ⓑ 3 ⓒ
4 ⓑ 5 founding

6 ⓒ 7 ⓓ 8 ⓐ
9 ⓑ 10 ⓔ

p. 50

Listening Skills Practice: Chronological Order I

A ⓐ 2 ⓑ 1 ⓒ 3

B

Script

M Teacher: The *Iliad* and *Odyssey* are two epic poems written by the Greek Homer. They tell about the Trojan War and what happened afterward. There's another epic poem that focuses on the events after the Trojan War. It's the *Aeneid*. The Roman Virgil wrote the poem. The *Aeneid* tells the story of Aeneas. He was one of the greatest heroes of Troy. He was also the ancestor of the Roman people.

According to the *Aeneid*, Aeneas and a group of followers escaped from Troy while the Greeks were destroying it. They sailed in the Mediterranean Sea. They wound up in Africa at the city of Carthage. Queen Dido of Carthage fell in love with Aeneas. But Aeneas realized he had to sail away to fulfill his destiny. His destiny was to be the father of a great and powerful race of people. Eventually, Aeneas landed in Italy. He married Lavinia, killed his rival Turnus, and became the father of the Roman people.

1 ⓑ
2 ⓒ
3 ⓐ 2 ⓑ 3 ⓒ 1

Unit 10 The Roman Republic

p. 51

Pre-Listening Questions Sample Answer

1 I can see a statue of a man. I don't know who he is though. And I can see the Colosseum.
2 It was more than 2,000 years ago.
3 Rome became a great power during that time. And it controlled most of the area in the Mediterranean Sea.
4 There were different social classes in the Choson Dynasty. They were *yangban*, *jungin*, *sangmin*, and *chunmin*. *Yangban* referred to people in the noble class, but *chunmin* referred to people at the very bottom of society, like slaves called *nobi*.

Vocabulary

1 monarchy	2 peasant
3 legend	4 represent
5 territory	6 elect

p. 52

Script

M Teacher: According to legend, Rome was founded in 753 B.C. The first ruler of Rome was Romulus, the city's founder. For around 240 years, Rome was ruled by kings. However, some Romans decided that they didn't want to be ruled by kings. So the wealthy aristocrats and poor peasants worked together. They got rid of the monarchy. In 509 B.C., Rome became a republic.

A republic is a type of representative government. The Romans elected people to serve in the Roman Senate. These senators represented the will of the people. Over time, the Romans developed a number of elected positions. This helped stabilize the government.

Because Rome was united, it grew stronger. The Romans began to expand their power. The Roman army slowly started conquering cities throughout the Italian peninsula. This happened around 400 B.C. By 264 B.C., Rome ruled most of the Italian peninsula.

That was also the year that the First Punic War began. As Rome gained power, it came into conflict with other powers in the Mediterranean region. One was Carthage. Carthage was located in North Africa. Rome fought three wars with Carthage. Rome won the Third Punic War in 146 B.C. and destroyed Carthage. This opened much of the rest of the Mediterranean region to Rome.

Rome's territory quickly expanded. It seized land in the areas that are modern-day Spain, France, and Greece. It ruled land in the Middle East and Northern Africa, too. Eventually, though, some of the most powerful men in Rome fought one another. This led to a civil war. The Roman Republic ended in 27 B.C. when Augustus Caesar was named the emperor. This started the time of the Roman Empire.

Organizer

ⓐ republic	ⓑ representative
ⓒ 264 B.C.	ⓓ Carthage
ⓔ Europe	ⓕ emperor

p. 53

Comprehension

1 ⓐ	2 ⓑ	3 ⓒ
4 ⓒ	5 founded	
6 ⓐ	7 ⓔ	8 ⓒ
9 ⓑ	10 ⓓ	

p. 54

Listening Skills Practice: Chronological Order II

A ⓐ 1 ⓑ 3 ⓒ 2

B

Script

M Student: For my report on Romans from the Roman Republic, I chose Cincinnatus. He lived during the fifth century B.C. Cincinnatus served as a consul in Rome in 460 B.C. But he didn't enjoy political life. Instead, he preferred to spend time on his farm. In 458 B.C., the Romans were in a war with a group of people called the Aequi. The Aequi defeated a Roman army. The Roman Senate became very worried. They appointed Cincinnatus dictator of Rome for six months. Cincinnatus learned about his new job while he was plowing a field. He didn't want the power, but he accepted it. Cincinnatus went to Rome, led the army, and battled the Aequi. He quickly defeated them. After that, he gave up power sixteen days after the Senate gave it to him. He didn't want to rule at all. Then, he returned to his farm. Because of his actions, Cincinnatus was one of the greatest Romans in history. He had enormous power but willingly gave it up.

1 ⓐ
2 ⓑ
3 ⓐ sixteen, 3
ⓑ 458 B.C., 2
ⓒ 460 B.C., 1

Unit 11 Julius Caesar

p. 55

Pre-Listening Questions Sample Answer

1 Julius Caesar was a great Roman general.
2 A group of Romans stabbed him with knives.
3 Caesar conquered Gaul. He also tried to help the poor people in Rome.
4 Emperor Hadrian built a wall in England. Emperor Nero did many strange things. Brutus was one of the men who killed Caesar.

Vocabulary

1	beat	2	corruption
3	plot	4	orator
5	stab	6	senator

p. 56

Script

W Teacher: Julius Caesar was one of the greatest men of the Roman Republic. He was accomplished in several fields. He was a lawyer and orator. Some said his speaking skills were similar to Cicero's. Cicero was considered the best Roman orator. Caesar held many positions in the government. He was a talented writer. And he was a brilliant general.

Julius Caesar was born in 100 B.C. When he was growing up, the Roman Republic had many problems. There was a lot of government corruption. This caused the republic to go into decline. After becoming an adult, Caesar was elected to several government positions. He fought corruption. He suggested new laws for the Senate to pass. He also tried to help the poor people in Rome have better lives.

When he was forty-one, he became the governor of Gaul. Gaul was the ancient name of France. In Gaul, Caesar was in charge of a Roman army. He fought many battles in Gaul. He always defeated his enemies. Tribes from Germany and other areas attacked his armies. But Caesar beat them as well. By then, he had become one of the empire's most powerful men.

As Caesar gained more power, the Roman Senate got worried. The senators feared Caesar would seize power. They were right. In 49 B.C., Caesar entered Rome with his army. He took over the government. Most of the poor people were happy. But the senators were upset. Caesar made lots of changes in Rome. Many senators disliked these changes. So some of them plotted to kill Caesar. On March 15, 44 B.C., several men stabbed Caesar with knives and killed him when he entered the Senate.

Organizer

ⓐ accomplished
ⓑ corruption
ⓒ took over
ⓓ changes
ⓔ plotted against
ⓕ March 15

p. 57

Comprehension

1 ⓒ 2 ⓐ 3 ⓑ
4 ⓑ 5 killed

6 ⓓ 7 ⓐ 8 ⓑ
9 ⓔ 10 ⓒ

p. 58

Listening Skills Practice: Problem and Solution I

A ⓐ P ⓑ P ⓒ S
B

Script

M Teacher: After Julius Caesar was killed, there was a struggle for power in Rome. Three men decided to share power. They were Mark Antony, Lepidus, and Octavian. Octavian was the nephew of Julius Caesar as well as his heir. This period was called the Second Triumvirate. After a while, the three men began fighting with one another. Each one wanted to be the only ruler of Rome. Octavian's troops fought and defeated the army of Lepidus. Then, Lepidus's men joined Octavian's side. Mark Antony suddenly needed an ally. He found an ally in Egypt. He joined forces with Cleopatra of Egypt. In 31 B.C., there was a great naval battle. It was called the Battle of Actium. Octavian defeated Antony and Cleopatra. One year later, both Antony and Cleopatra committed suicide. That made Octavian the most powerful man in Rome. In 27 B.C., the Senate gave Octavian a new title: emperor. He changed his name to Augustus Caesar. And he became the first leader of the Roman Empire.

1 ⓒ

2 ⓑ

3 ⓐ Three men decided to share power.
ⓑ He joined forces with Cleopatra in Egypt.

Unit 12 The Fall of the Roman Empire

p. 59

Pre-Listening Questions Sample Answer

1 It fell sometime in the fifth century.

2 Some barbarians from Germany defeated the Roman Empire.

3 The empire became corrupt. There were many problems in the empire. And the barbarian tribes around the empire grew more powerful.

4 It lasted for almost 500 years. There were many great emperors during that time. The Roman Empire was the greatest empire in history.

Vocabulary

1	steal	2	big
3	tribe	4	politician
5	split	6	antiquity

p. 60

Script

M Teacher: The Roman Empire started in 27 B.C. It lasted until 476 A.D. During that time, Rome expanded a great deal. At its height, it controlled most of Southern and Central Europe, parts of Britain, and much of North Africa and the Middle East. It was the largest empire in antiquity. And Rome was the world's most important city.

All empires eventually fall though. This was the case for Rome. Rome lost power and fell for several reasons. A big reason involved Emperor Diocletian. In 285, he decided that the Roman Empire was too large and impossible for one person to rule. So he split the empire into two. He created the Western Roman Empire and the Eastern Roman Empire. Rome remained the capital in the west. The capital in the east became Constantinople. Much of Rome's wealth went east. This weakened the western empire.

At the same time, several barbarian tribes in the west gained power. These tribes included the Visigoths, Vandals, and Franks. They often fought and defeated the Roman legions. This caused the Western Roman Empire to lose land. The politicians in Rome were weak and corrupt, too. They stole money from Rome to improve their own lives. Doing that caused harm to Rome.

In 410, a Germanic army of Visigoths invaded Rome. The army destroyed lots of buildings and stole many treasures. Rome wasn't captured though. Then, in 476, another Germanic army attacked Rome. The army's leader was Odoacer. His army captured Rome. Odoacer made Emperor Romulus Augustulus give up the throne. He was the last Roman emperor. So historians say that the fall of the Roman Empire happened in 476.

Organizer

ⓐ eastern and western　ⓑ wealth
ⓒ Politicians　ⓓ Barbarian
ⓔ 410　ⓕ fell

p. 61

Comprehension

1	ⓒ	2	ⓑ	3	ⓑ
4	ⓒ	5	emperor		
6	ⓐ	7	ⓔ	8	ⓓ
9	ⓒ	10	ⓑ		

p. 62

Listening Skills Practice: Problem and Solution II

A ⓐ S　ⓑ P　ⓒ P

B

Script

W Student: I did my report on the Byzantine Empire. It was formed from the Eastern Roman Empire. The first Byzantine emperor was Constantine I. People often call him Constantine the Great. He ruled from 306 to 337. When he became the emperor, he had no capital city. So he built a great city. It was called Constantinople. It's Istanbul, Turkey, today. Constantinople became the greatest city in the world. It remained the capital of the Byzantine Empire for more than 1,000 years. The empire lasted until the year 1453. While the Byzantine Empire existed, it often fought wars against Muslim invaders. The Muslims were attempting to get into Europe. They often had powerful armies. But the Byzantines managed to defeat them for hundreds of years. Over time, though, the empire lost power. In the 1400s, it became very weak. Finally, a huge army of Ottoman Turks captured Constantinople in 1453. This resulted in the end of the Byzantine Empire.

1 ⓑ
2 ⓐ
3 ⓐ He built a great city called Constantinople.
ⓑ The Byzantines fought against them for hundreds of years.

Chapter 4 Art and Artists

Unit 13 Realism

p. 65

Pre-Listening Questions Sample Answer

1 It shows people, places, and things just as they look in real life.
2 I guess it was more than 100 years ago.
3 I don't know any of their names.
4 Manet was an Impressionist. Picasso made all kinds of art.

Vocabulary

1 everyday
2 detest
3 precisely
4 reaction
5 complain
6 landscape

p. 66

Script

W Teacher: At the end of the 1700s, a new movement began. People called it the Romantic Movement. It influenced many different fields, including art. The art of the Romantic Era stressed emotions and feelings. Imagination and mystery were also important to the art of this time. The Romantic Era lasted until the mid-1800s. By then, artists were getting tired of it. They wanted to create a new style of art.

This new style was called Realism. It lasted from about 1840 to 1880. Realism was a reaction to Romanticism. So the two styles of art were very different. First of all, Realist artists paid very close attention to details. They tried to paint their subjects precisely as they looked in real life. Next, Realist artists painted pictures of everyday people and events. For example, they painted farmers working in their fields. Others painted people eating food or made landscapes with animals in them. Realist artists didn't have any important message in their art. They simply wanted to show the world as it existed.

There were a lot of famous artists from this time. Gustave Courbet was one. Honore Daumier and Winslow Homer were two others. The Realist Era lasted for around four decades. But it wasn't popular with everyone. Art critics often complained that the scenes were ugly. They thought Realist artists didn't make the people in their paintings look good. The upper class frequently detested Realist art. Realist paintings often showed how poor the members of the lower classes were. Yet many other people liked the art of this era. Today, paintings from that period sell for large amounts of money.

Organizer

ⓐ 1880
ⓑ reaction
ⓒ real life
ⓓ everyday
ⓔ Winslow Homer
ⓕ upper class

p. 67

Comprehension

1 ⓑ
2 ⓑ
3 ⓒ
4 ⓒ
5 Romantic

6 ⓑ
7 ⓔ
8 ⓐ
9 ⓓ
10 ⓒ

p. 68

Listening Skills Practice: Summarizing I

A ⓐ

B

Script

W Teacher: Edouard Manet was born in Paris, France, in 1832. All his life, he wanted to be an artist. He grew up during the Realist Period, so he learned to paint that type of art. He traveled all around Europe to look at artwork and to learn from it. He then began painting. One of his first paintings was *The Absinthe Drinker*. It showed a poor man drinking. He submitted it to the Salon, the official art exhibition in France. But his painting was turned down. Later, he submitted another painting. But it was rejected as well. The rejections upset him, so he changed his style. Around that time, the Impressionist Movement was starting in France. The Impressionists used bright colors. They painted with broad brushstrokes. Manet adopted these methods. He continued to paint scenes from everyday life. Finally, some of his paintings were accepted by the Salon. That helped him become famous during his life. By that time, he had changed from a Realist artist to an Impressionist.

1 ⓐ　2 ⓒ　3 ⓑ

Unit 14 Dutch Golden Age Painting

p. 69

Pre-Listening Questions Sample Answer

1 It was more than 300 years ago.
2 They had a very strong economy, so life in the Netherlands was good then.
3 Rembrandt was one. I don't know any others.
4 I know they made religious paintings and portraits. I'm not sure what else they made.

Vocabulary

1 patron　2 enormous
3 etching　4 prolific
5 incredibly　6 wealthy

p. 70

Script

M Teacher: In the 1600s, England, France, and Spain were all great powers in Europe. Another much smaller country was also a great power. This country was the Netherlands. The Netherlands, or Holland, is a small country in Western Europe. It lies to the west of Germany and is near France. To the north is the North Sea. In the 1600s, the Netherlands was incredibly powerful and wealthy. Despite only having two million people, the Dutch had a global empire. Due to their enormous wealth, many Dutch people became patrons of the arts. This led to a period called Dutch Golden Age Painting.

During the 1600s, Dutch artists were very prolific. Some art historians believe that Dutch artists created up to five million paintings during this period. Dutch artists made all kinds of paintings. They often focused on portraits, still-lifes, and genre paintings. Genre paintings show scenes from everyday life. Other Dutch artists painted historical scenes and landscapes.

The most famous artist from this time was Rembrandt. He painted hundreds of paintings and also made etchings and drawings. He made all kinds of paintings, including ones with religious themes. His paintings are quite striking and tend to use dark colors. *Christ in the Storm* and *The Blinding of Samson* are two of his well-known religious paintings. *The Night Watch* is another famous painting by Rembrandt. Jan Vermeer was another great artist from that time. He painted fewer pictures than Rembrandt, but art historians still call him a master painter. Frans Hals and Jan Steen were two other noted artists from this time.

Organizer

ⓐ 1600s　ⓑ The Netherlands
ⓒ patrons　ⓓ five
ⓔ genre paintings　ⓕ Rembrandt

p. 71

Comprehension

1 ⓐ　2 ⓒ　3 ⓒ
4 ⓑ　5 master painter

6 ⓒ　7 ⓐ　8 ⓔ
9 ⓓ　10 ⓑ

p. 72

Listening Skills Practice: Summarizing II

A ⓒ

B

Script

M Documentary Narrator: Rembrandt van Rijn was a Dutch artist. After Vincent van Gogh, he's probably the best-known painter from the Netherlands. Rembrandt was born in 1606 and died in 1669. During his life, he created more than 600 paintings. He also made many etchings and around 2,000 drawings. Rembrandt was a natural artist. He opened an art studio at the age of nineteen and started teaching art just two years later. Rembrandt painted many genres of art. He loved painting portraits. He made numerous self-portraits as well as portraits of other people. Some of the people whose portraits he painted were his parents. He painted pictures with religious themes. He also made landscapes and cityscapes. Some of his paintings, like *The Night Watch*, were enormous. That painting is more than four meters long and three meters tall. Others are much smaller. During our program tonight, we're going to look closely at a variety of Rembrandt's works. We hope you enjoy the show.

1 ⓒ 2 ⓑ 3 ⓑ

Unit 15 Frederic Remington

p. 73

Pre-Listening Questions Sample Answer

1 I can see a statue of a cowboy on a horse. And the other picture shows some soldiers with their horses.
2 He was an American artist.
3 He made art that showed scenes from the American West.
4 I like both Realist and Impressionist art.

Vocabulary

1 ranching 2 sketching
3 watercolor 4 unsettled
5 untamed 6 sculpture

p. 74

Script

M Teacher: In the 1800s, the majority of Americans lived east of the Mississippi River. The western part of the country was mostly unsettled. It was an untamed, dangerous land. There were lots of wild animals such as grizzly bears, buffalo, and wolves. There were Indians who often made war against settlers. The West was also fascinating to most people in the eastern part of the country.

One of the people interested in the West was Frederic Remington. Born in 1861, he made his first trip to the West when he was nineteen years old. Remington enjoyed doing outdoor activities. He liked hunting, fishing, and hiking. He tried ranching out West. He was also an artist.

In his early twenties, Remington began sketching and drawing pictures of scenes in the West. He sold some of his pictures to the magazine *Harper's Weekly*. They were an instant success. The American public was intrigued by the pictures. They wanted more. Remington quickly realized he could make a career out of being an artist.

Remington created several types of art. He painted with both watercolors and oils. He drew pictures. And he made sculptures as well. He used the realist and impressionist styles for his work. He often created artwork featuring cowboys and Indians. He made many pictures of the U.S. Cavalry as well. His works often showed the scenery of the American West as well. One of his most famous works was the sculpture *The Bronco Buster*. It shows a cowboy riding a horse that's standing on its back two legs. He made several of these sculptures. One of the original sculptures is in the Oval Office in the White House.

Organizer

ⓐ unsettled ⓑ fascinating
ⓒ wild animals ⓓ successful
ⓔ Indians ⓕ sculptures

p. 75

Comprehension

1 ⓐ 2 ⓒ 3 ⓑ
4 ⓐ 5 outdoor activities

6 ⓓ 7 ⓑ 8 ⓔ
9 ⓐ 10 ⓒ

p. 76

Listening Skills Practice: **Note-Taking I**

A ⓐ The western part of the country was mostly unsettled. It was an untamed, dangerous land.

ⓑ In his early twenties, Remington began sketching and drawing pictures of scenes in the West.

ⓒ He painted with both watercolors and oils. He drew pictures. And he made sculptures as well.

B

Script

M Teacher: Many people believe art is only something that people draw, paint, or sculpt. But that's not true. There are many other kinds of art as well. For example, photography is one kind of art. This involves making art with a camera. One of the greatest photographers ever was Ansel Adams.

Ansel Adams was born in San Francisco, California, in 1902. In 1916, he went on a family trip to Yosemite National Park in California. Yosemite is considered one of the most beautiful places in the United States. There, Adams took some of his first amateur photos. He also fell in love with the park. He returned to it many times in his life. At Yosemite, he not only took photos but also worked to help preserve the park so that future generations could enjoy it.

Adams went on to become a professional photographer. He often used black-and-white film for his pictures. He loved to take pictures of landscapes. Some of the photos he took are simply breathtaking.

1 ⓐ

2 ⓑ

3 ⓐ one kind of art, involves making art with a camera

ⓑ in California, one of most beautiful places in U.S.

ⓒ used black-and-white film for pictures, took pictures of landscapes

Unit 16 Vincent van Gogh

p. 77

Pre-Listening Questions Sample Answer

1 They are both paintings by van Gogh. The first one is *Starry Night*, and the other one is a self-portrait he painted.

2 He was one of the greatest painters in history.

3 He made Impressionist art.

4 I love van Gogh's art. I also like Cezanne and Monet. I like the Impressionists very much.

Vocabulary

1	period	2	genius
3	vibrant	4	masterpiece
5	productive	6	major

p. 78

Script

M Teacher: One of history's greatest artists only sold one painting during his entire life. And he sold that painting just a few months before he died. During his life, his paintings were commercial failures. His brother even owned an art gallery and tried to sell the paintings. No one was interested in purchasing them. After he died, though, people changed their minds about his work. They realized that this man had been an artistic genius. Today, his paintings sell for millions of dollars. The name of this artist is Vincent van Gogh.

Van Gogh had a difficult life. He often had little or no money. As a result, he had to borrow money from his brother. He battled mental illness for much of his life. This caused him to cut off part of his ear and to commit suicide when he was thirty-seven years old. He also had little formal training as an artist.

Still, he loved drawing and painting. During his life, he was incredibly productive. He created more than 2,000 works of art in his life. Around 900 of them were paintings. He sometimes completed masterpieces in a single day. Van Gogh's first major work was *The Potato Eaters*. He finished it in 1885. That was from his first period as an artist. *The Potato Eaters* used very dark colors. But van Gogh's style changed later in his life. He began painting with vibrant bright colors. He used this style for his painting *Starry Night*. It is one of the most recognizable works of art in the world. Van Gogh painted it in 1889. A year later, in 1890, he killed himself, and the art world lost a genius.

Organizer

ⓐ money	ⓑ mental illness
ⓒ one	ⓓ 900
ⓕ major	ⓔ *Starry Night*

p. 79

Comprehension

1 ⓐ 2 ⓑ 3 ⓐ
4 ⓑ 5 millions of dollars

6 ⓒ 7 ⓐ 8 ⓑ
9 ⓔ 10 ⓓ

p. 80

Listening Skills Practice: Note-Taking II

A ⓐ This caused him to cut off part of his ear and to commit suicide when he was thirty-seven years old.
ⓑ He created more than 2,000 works of art in his life. Around 900 of them were paintings.
ⓒ But van Gogh's style changed later in his life. He began painting with vibrant bright colors.

B

Script

W Art Gallery Guide: Thank you for coming to the Vincent van Gogh Museum. As you know, we are located in Amsterdam in the Netherlands. While Amsterdam wasn't van Gogh's hometown, he was Dutch. And we are proud to have a large number of his paintings here on exhibit. In fact, we have more than 200 of van Gogh's paintings here in the permanent exhibit. That is the largest collection of works by van Gogh in the entire world. We have a wide variety of his paintings. They include landscapes, self-portraits, portraits, and still-lifes. We also have many of his letters and drawings on exhibit. Finally, the museum has some works of his that other museums and collectors have loaned to us. These works come from every period in van Gogh's art career. So you will get to see a wide range of his works. I think you'll be impressed with our collection. So let's begin our tour right now. Here's the first painting I'd like to show you.

1 ⓒ
2 ⓑ
3 ⓐ Amsterdam, Netherlands
ⓑ 200 paintings, largest collection in world
ⓒ landscapes, self-portraits, portraits, and still-lifes

Chapter 5 The Environment

Unit 17 Pollution

p. 83

Pre-Listening Questions Sample Answer

1 I can see different kinds of pollution in each picture.
2 Pollution is anything that makes the air, land, or ground dirty.
3 People cause pollution. Garbage and chemicals cause pollution, too.
4 We can prevent pollution by caring more about the environment and not littering.

Vocabulary

1 pollute 2 landfill
3 soil 4 waterway
5 manmade 6 fertilizer

p. 84

Script

W Teacher: When a person adds something harmful to the environment, that individual is creating pollution. There are several kinds of pollution. But there are three main types. They are air, water, and soil pollution.

Air pollution affects the air that humans breathe. Most air pollution is manmade. It comes from many sources. The two major sources of pollution are factories and vehicles. Factories often release harmful chemicals into the air. So do vehicles like cars, buses, and trucks. Factories and vehicles create a lot of air pollution since they burn fossil fuels. These are sources of energy such as oil, coal, and gas. Oil and coal are quite dirty, so they're responsible for a great deal of air pollution.

Water pollution is a major problem in many places, too. Water pollution makes clean water dirty. As a result, people and animals can't drink the water. In addition, fish, other animals, and even plants can't live in polluted water. Sadly, humans cause a lot of water pollution. Some people dump garbage and chemicals into water sources. Other times, fertilizer that farmers use gets into waterways. Oil spills can create water pollution, too. All of these things greatly harm the Earth's oceans, seas, rivers, and lakes.

The third major type is soil pollution. This happens when the ground gets polluted. Once again, humans cause very much soil pollution. Farmers can pollute the soil by using insecticide to kill insects. Miners can harm the ground by mining the land in certain ways. And places such as landfills, where people take their garbage, can cause a large amount of soil pollution.

Organizer

ⓐ vehicles
ⓑ fossil fuels
ⓒ Water
ⓓ fertilizer
ⓔ miners
ⓓ landfills

p. 85

Comprehension

1 ⓐ
2 ⓒ
3 ⓑ
4 ⓐ
5 harmful
6 ⓐ
7 ⓒ
8 ⓔ
9 ⓑ
10 ⓓ

p. 86

Listening Skills Practice: Classification I

A ⓐ factories and vehicles
ⓑ fossil fuels
ⓒ dumping garbage
ⓓ oil spills
ⓔ the ground
ⓕ farmers and miners

B

Script

W Teacher: Pollution has made many parts of the world both dirty and unhealthy. Fortunately, there are many ways for humans to improve the environment. So we can make pollution less of a problem. One major way to do that is to use gas-powered vehicles less often. Cars, buses, and trucks create lots of air pollution. They do that because they burn gas. People can create less air pollution by taking buses, subways, and other forms of mass transportation. People can also buy electric cars. These cars don't have gas engines, so they don't pollute the environment by burning gasoline. Water pollution is another big problem. We can reduce water pollution in a couple of ways. First, farmers can use less fertilizer in their fields. Then, the rain will not wash so much fertilizer into waterways. Next, we can reduce the number of oil spills in the ocean. By doing those two activities, we can keep the water clean.

1 ⓑ
2 ⓐ
3 ⓐ gas-powered vehicles
ⓑ mass transportation
ⓒ electric cars
ⓓ less fertilizer
ⓔ the number of oil spills

Unit 18 Natural Resources

p. 87

Pre-Listening Questions Sample Answer

1 I can see different types of natural resources. There are water, trees, gold, and silver in the pictures.
2 They are resources that come from the Earth.
3 We use them to eat, to make things with, and to create energy.
4 Yes, we should. Many natural resources are not unlimited. So we need to use them carefully.

Vocabulary

1 biotic
2 abundant
3 conserve
4 abiotic
5 replace
6 category

p. 88

Script

M Teacher: Anything that is not manmade is a natural resource. There are all kinds of them. Some are living. Those are biotic resources. Others are not living. Those are abiotic resources. Biotic resources include trees, domestic animals such as cows and sheep, wild animals, and fish. A few abiotic resources are metals, water, and air. Some natural resources are highly valuable to humans. Others aren't valuable at all.

There are differing amounts of natural resources on the Earth. So, while there's plenty of air, there are small amounts of rare metals. In addition, there are two primary categories of natural resources: renewable resources and nonrenewable resources.

Renewable resources can be replaced fairly easily. Or they never run out. For instance, there's an endless supply of sunlight. Air, wind, and water are also abundant.

Thus people can use them again and again. Trees, fruits, and vegetables are renewable resources. People can grow them fairly quickly. Animals are renewable resources, too. For example, cows, sheep, chickens, pigs, and other farm animals reproduce.

On the other hand, nonrenewable resources are limited in supply. Coal, oil, and gas are fossil fuels. They produce most of the energy that people use. Yet there are limited supplies of all three. It takes millions of years for them to be produced. Once they are burned to make energy, they cannot be used again. Gold, silver, iron, and other metals are also nonrenewable resources. There are finite supplies of all of them. Thus people need to conserve them so that they don't run out.

Organizer

ⓐ run out
ⓑ sunlight
ⓒ reproduce
ⓓ in supply
ⓔ fossil fuels
ⓕ be conserved

p. 89

Comprehension

1 ⓐ
2 ⓐ
3 ⓒ
4 ⓑ
5 Nonrenewable

6 ⓑ
7 ⓒ
8 ⓐ
9 ⓔ
10 ⓓ

p. 90

Listening Skills Practice: Classification II

A ⓐ never run out
ⓑ air, wind, and water
ⓒ fruits, and vegetables
ⓓ limited
ⓔ coal, oil, and gas
ⓕ silver, iron

B

Script

M News Announcer: For many years, environmentalists have been claiming that the Earth is running out of fossil fuels. Many of them have even declared that the Earth's oil supply will be gone in a few years. As it turns out, these environmentalists were all wrong. The Earth's oil supply is actually increasing.

Nowadays, geologists are discovering new fields of oil all over the Earth. One reason is that modern technology has improved a lot. For example, geologists now know that there are vast oil fields deep beneath the Arctic Ocean. In addition, advances in technology now let people get oil from new places. In the United States and Canada, there are many shale oil fields. These are rocks with oil in them. Likewise, geologists can now remove oil from oil sands. In the past, that wasn't possible. There are shale oil fields and oil sands in many places on the Earth. Thanks to these new discoveries and improved technology, the Earth isn't going to run out of oil for a long, long time.

1 ⓑ
2 ⓒ
3 ⓐ modern technology
ⓑ the Arctic Ocean
ⓒ shale oil
ⓓ sands
ⓔ remove oil from

Unit 19 Recycling

p. 91

Pre-Listening Questions Sample Answer

1 They are holding recycling bins.
2 Recycling is using things again so that you don't have to throw them away.
3 People can recycle paper, glass, metal, and plastic objects.
4 I think it is good to recycle some products because it can help the environment and reduce the amount of trash people produce.

Vocabulary

1 merely
2 reuse
3 preserve
4 limited
5 overflowing
6 sort

p. 92

Script

M Teacher: These days, most people don't merely put all of their trash into one bag and then throw it away. They sort their trash now. Thus they don't throw certain items away. Instead, they set these items aside so that they can be recycled. Recycling is a great way to reuse some products. There are many items people can recycle. Paper, plastic, glass, and metal products can all be recycled. It's possible to recycle electronics and textiles, too.

There are numerous benefits to recycling. First of all, it allows people to preserve precious natural resources. This is especially true of metal and paper products. The amount of metals in the ground is limited. By recycling products such as aluminum cans, people can reduce the amount of metals that need to be mined from the ground. Likewise, by recycling paper, people will be able to cut down fewer trees.

Another benefit of recycling is that people will produce less garbage if they recycle. Landfills are enormous places where people dispose of their garbage. Unfortunately, lots of these landfills are overflowing. There's too much trash in them. By recycling, people can reduce the amount of trash that's taken to landfills. As a result, landfills will fill up more slowly.

By recycling, people can also reduce the amount of pollution on the planet. For instance, many electronics and batteries have chemicals in them. These chemicals can leak into the ground. But, if people recycle them, then these items won't pollute the soil. Thus, by recycling, people can make sure that the Earth is cleaner and healthier.

Organizer

ⓐ reuse　ⓑ metal products
ⓒ textiles　ⓓ valuable
ⓔ less garbage　ⓕ soil

p. 93

Comprehension

1 ⓑ　2 ⓐ　3 ⓑ
4 ⓒ　5 glass

6 ⓓ　7 ⓐ　8 ⓑ
9 ⓒ　10 ⓔ

p. 94

Listening Skills Practice: Understanding Organization I

A ⓐ ⓘ　ⓑ ⓘ

B

Script

W Teacher: You've probably noticed the recycling logo on various products. It has three green arrows on it. The arrows are pointed so that they're going around in a circle. This is known as the Recycling Loop. There are three stages in it. They are collecting, processing, and buying. The first stage is collecting. In this stage, people collect materials that are recyclable. There are all kinds of materials to collect. These include newspapers, plastic bottles, aluminum cans, and glassware. Once people collect materials, they can take them to a recycling center. This is the processing stage. The items are sorted according to what type of material they are made from. Then, they're sold to various companies. These companies make the products into new items. Finally, the new items are taken to stores. There, people can buy them. By buying recycled products, people can show their support for recycling. And they can make sure that companies will continue to recycle products in the future.

1 ⓐ　2 ⓒ　3 ⓐ

Unit 20 Renewable Energy

p. 95

Pre-Listening Questions Sample Answer

1 I can see a house with solar panels in the first picture. And I can see a dam in the second picture.
2 It is an energy source that can be used again and again.
3 People can use the wind, sunlight, and water to produce renewable energy.
4 It's clean and can be used again and again. Unfortunately, you can't use it everywhere. It's not very efficient. And wind turbines kill lots of birds, so I don't like them.

Vocabulary

1 volcanic　2 fragile
3 inefficient　4 maintenance
5 blade　6 practical

p. 96

Script

W Teacher: Around the world, fossil fuels provide more than eighty percent of people's energy needs. The main ones are coal, oil, and gas. They are very efficient and fairly cheap. But there is a limited supply of them. Thus they are nonrenewable energy sources. The fossil fuel supply will run out in the future. So people are looking for new energy sources. Many are turning to renewable energy.

Renewable energy can be used again and again. The supply of it won't run out. There are several types of renewable energy. They include solar power, hydroelectric power, wind power, tidal power, and geothermal power.

Solar power comes from the sun. Hydroelectric power comes from running water in rivers. Wind power uses the wind to make energy. Tidal power uses the power of ocean tides to make energy. And geothermal power uses the heat from deep within the Earth to make energy.

There are many advantages to renewable energy. First, it won't run out. Second, it's very clean. It creates little or no pollution. Third, the facilities that create electricity often require little maintenance. So they're cheap and easy to run.

There are some disadvantages to them though. For instance, they can't be used everywhere. Solar energy isn't practical in cloudy places. Geothermal energy can only be used in regions with volcanic activity. At the present time, they are inefficient and expensive, too. Finally, they can have negative effects on their regions. Many wind turbines kill lots of birds with their blades. And dams over rivers can upset fragile ecosystems.

Organizer

ⓐ different ⓑ hydroelectric
ⓒ run out ⓓ clean
ⓔ everywhere ⓕ negative

p. 97

Comprehension

1 ⓒ 2 ⓐ 3 ⓐ
4 ⓑ 5 fossil fuels

6 ⓑ 7 ⓓ 8 ⓐ
9 ⓔ 10 ⓒ

p. 98

Listening Skills Practice: Understanding Organization II

A ⓐ ⓘⓘ ⓑ ⓘ
B

Script

M Hydroelectric Power Plant Employee: Welcome, everyone, to the Walters Dam. The Walters Dam lies across the Western River. There's a hydroelectric power plant here at the dam. It creates electricity for people in the local area. The dam provides several benefits. Let me tell you about them. First, the power plant creates cheap and clean electricity. Thanks to the running water of the Western River, the power plant makes electricity all day and night long. Local residents can get as much electricity as they need. Their electric bills have even decreased since the dam opened. The dam doesn't pollute the air like coal-fired power plants do. So the air is nice and clean to breathe. The lake behind Walters Dam also provides many benefits. People can enjoy swimming, boating, and fishing on the lake. Finally, don't worry about how the dam affects salmon swimming upriver to lay their eggs. There are fish ladders that the salmon can use to get past the dam. So the dam doesn't harm the local wildlife at all.

1 ⓑ 2 ⓒ 3 ⓐ

Word List

Word List

Chapter 1 Natural Disasters

Unit 01

1 **damage** *(n)* harm
You should not cause any ***damage*** to the store.

2 **disaster** *(n)* an event in which great harm is done
It was a ***disaster*** when the building suddenly collapsed.

3 **expel** *(v)* to throw out
The principal ***expelled*** the bad student from school.

4 **island** *(n)* land that is surrounded by water on all of its sides
We will spend our vacation on a tropical ***island*** in Hawaii.

5 **minor** *(adj)* small; not important
Make a few ***minor*** changes to the report, please.

6 **powerfully** *(adv)* in a strong manner or way
John spoke ***powerfully*** about the need for change.

7 **rise** *(v)* to come up; to go up
All of the students ***rise*** when the teacher enters the room.

8 **sunrise** *(n)* the time when the sun comes up in the morning
Sunrise will take place at 6:10 this morning.

9 **sunset** *(n)* the time when the sun goes down at night
We love to see the ***sunset*** when we are at the beach.

10 **village** *(n)* a very small town
My grandparents live in a small ***village*** in the country.

Unit 02

1 **actually** *(adv)* really; in reality
Actually, Mr. Taylor is the owner of the company.

2 **aftershock** *(n)* a small earthquake that happens after a larger one
Some of the ***aftershocks*** were almost as big as the first earthquake.

3 **coast** *(n)* the land next to a large body of water
They are going to visit the ***coast*** to relax at the beach.

4 **continental** *(adj)* relating to a continent
The ***continental*** United States stretches from one ocean to another.

5 **crust** *(n)* the upper layer of the Earth
The ***crust*** of the Earth is several kilometers thick in most places.

6 **fault** *(n)* a long crack in the Earth's crust
A lot of times, earthquakes take place along ***faults*** in the crust.

7 **geologist** *(n)* a person who studies the Earth
Janet wants to be ***geologist*** when she gets older.

8 **imagine** *(v)* to think of; to dream of
I can't ***imagine*** what life would be like without computers.

9 **sink** *(v)* to go down beneath the surface
The ship began to ***sink*** when a hole appeared in the bottom of it.

10 **tremor** *(n)* a small earthquake
There was a minor ***tremor*** here around five minutes ago.

Unit 03

1 **astronomer** *(n)* a person who studies the stars, planets, and everything else in outer space

The ***astronomer*** is looking at the moon through his telescope.

2 **crater** *(n)* a large hole, often caused by one object hitting another
There are numerous ***craters*** on the moon.

3 **date** *(v)* to determine how old something is
They will attempt to ***date*** the object they found.

4 **diameter** *(n)* the width of an object that is shaped like a circle
What is the ***diameter*** of that large oak tree?

5 **dominant** *(adj)* more powerful than anyone or anything else
That team is so ***dominant*** that it wins the championship every year.

6 **dust** *(n)* very tiny particles of dirt
You need to clean your house to get rid of all of the ***dust***.

7 **enormous** *(adj)* huge; very large
A horse is large, but an elephant is ***enormous***.

8 **estimate** *(v)* to guess; to predict
I ***estimate*** that it will take six months to complete the project.

9 **handle** *(v)* to manage; to deal with
Mrs. Carter has a hard time ***handling*** all five of her children.

10 **shine** *(v)* to create light
Use the flashlight to ***shine*** some light over here.

Unit 04

1 **approach** *(v)* to go near
When you see the guard, do not ***approach*** any closer.

2 **donate** *(v)* to give money or something else to another person or group
You should ***donate*** money to charity every year.

3 **fear** *(v)* to be afraid; to be scared
Alice ***fears*** dogs so much that she won't even pet a tiny puppy.

4 **generator** *(n)* a machine that makes electricity
We use a ***generator*** when the power goes out during storms.

5 **hopefully** *(adv)* with luck; luckily
Hopefully, I will get a perfect grade on my test.

6 **inland** *(adj)* away from the water
Everyone is heading ***inland*** to avoid the coming typhoon.

7 **official** *(n)* a person who holds an elected or government office
The ***official*** is now in jail because he broke the law.

8 **rage** *(v)* to happen with great violence
The storm has been ***raging*** for three days.

9 **suffer** *(v)* to have something bad happen
She ***suffered*** terribly after she was in a car accident.

10 **town** *(n)* a small city
I grew up in a small ***town*** that had only 5,000 people.

Chapter 2 Fantasy Worlds

Unit 05

1 **brave** *(adj)* not having any fear; courageous
The ***brave*** soldiers did not run away during the battle.

2 **character** *(n)* a person in a play, movie, book, or other similar work
One of his favorite ***characters*** in the book is Aragorn.

3 **comedic** *(adj)* funny; humorous
The ***comedic*** scene made us laugh a lot.

4 **extremely** *(adv)* very; highly
The weather becomes ***extremely*** cold here in winter.

5 **horrible** *(adj)* awful; terrible; very bad
John was so ***horrible*** to his friends the other day.

6 **leader** *(n)* the person who is in charge of a group; the top person in a group
Peter is a natural ***leader***, so others are willing to follow him.

7 **manner** *(n)* a way; a method; a way of acting
Fred's ***manner*** is always very quiet and calm.

8 **memorable** *(adj)* easy to remember; excellent; unforgettable
Tell me about the most ***memorable*** event in your life.

9 **polite** *(adj)* having good manners; well behaved; behaving in a proper way
A gentlemen should always behave in a ***polite*** way.

10 **restore** *(v)* to bring back to one's original condition
Gabriel will attempt to ***restore*** the work of art.

Unit 06

1 **amazing** *(adj)* incredible; wonderful
Everyone agreed that the book they had just read was ***amazing***.

2 **basically** *(adv)* simply; mostly; essentially
Basically, you need to be nice to your friends.

3 **decade** *(n)* a period that last 10 years
They have been living on that farm for more than a ***decade***.

4 **deep** *(adj)* far into
We will go ***deep*** into the jungle on our trek.

5 **fearsome** *(adj)* scary; frightening
Sharks are some of the most ***fearsome*** creatures on the planet.

6 **force** *(n)* an army; a group of soldiers
A ***force*** of 100 men invaded the town.

7 **orc** *(n)* a goblin; a vicious monster
Orcs and dwarves are enemies in most fantasy stories.

8 **quest** *(n)* a mission to find or do something of importance
The ***quest*** of King Arthur's knights was to find the Holy Grail.

9 **scene** *(n)* a short part of a book, play, movie, or other similar work
What did you think of the final ***scene*** in the movie?

10 **trilogy** *(n)* a group of 3 books or movies related to one another
The first three *Star Wars* movies formed a ***trilogy***.

Unit 07

1 **being** *(n)* a creature
Some people believe there are ***beings*** from other planets on the Earth.

2 **detailed** *(adj)* complete; full; descriptive
Jim drew a ***detailed*** map for us to use.

3 **magical** *(adj)* possessing magic
That is a ***magical*** ring that can make its wearer invisible.

4 **novel** *(n)* a book of fiction
We have to read five ***novels*** during our summer vacation.

5 **primitive** *(adj)* simple; basic
Primitive humans lived in caves and did not farm the land,

6 **rerelease** *(v)* to show again at a movie theater
The studio is going to ***rerelease*** the film next month.

7 **star** *(v)* to feature a person in a movie, play, or television show
Peter is ***starring*** in the movie that just came out.

8 **tomb** *(n)* a place where someone is buried; a grave
The king was buried in a large ***tomb*** in the cemetery.

9 **true** *(adj)* real; actual
Please tell me the ***true*** story of what happened.

10 **wicked** *(adj)* evil; very bad
She is a ***wicked*** woman, so no one likes her.

Unit 08

1 **author** *(n)* a person who writes a book
Write a report about your favorite ***author***.

2 **currently** *(adv)* presently; now
Mary is ***currently*** taking a bus to the shopping mall.

3 **detective** *(n)* an investigator; a person who tries to solve mysteries
The ***detective*** is looking for clues to solve the robbery.

4 **encounter** *(n)* a meeting
How did your ***encounter*** with Brian go last night?

5 **guest** *(n)* a person who visits another person's home or place of business
We are going to have two ***guests*** for dinner tonight.

6 **highly** *(adv)* greatly; very much
He ***highly*** impressed all of us with his interview.

7 **lord** *(n)* a member of the nobility
That man is the ***lord*** of the village and all of the land around it.

8 **proceed** *(v)* to continue
You may ***proceed***, but please be careful.

9 **solve** *(v)* to find the answer to a problem
Let's try to ***solve*** the math problems in the book.

10 **troll** *(n)* a monster that is much larger than a human
Trolls are monsters that often live deep underground.

Chapter 3 The Roman Era

Unit 09

1 **afterward** *(adv)* later; at another time
Afterward, we are all going to meet at the restaurant for dinner.

2 **ancestor** *(n)* a person from whom another one is descended
Some people believe Adam is the ***ancestor*** of all humans.

3 **argue** *(v)* to fight verbally with someone
What were you and Tina ***arguing*** about?

4 **destiny** *(n)* fate; something that is going to happen to a person in the future
His ***destiny*** is to live in a foreign land for many years.

5 **escape** *(v)* to get away from
The criminals tried to ***escape*** from the police.

6 **follower** *(n)* a supporter; a person who belongs to a group led by someone else
The politician has a large number of ***followers***.

7 **fulfill** *(v)* to complete; to finish doing something
You must ***fulfill*** your promise before you do anything else.

8 **poem** *(n)* a work of literature written in verse
We read a ***poem*** by John Milton in class today.

9 **riverbank** *(n)* the area of land next to a river
There are some men fishing on the ***riverbank***.

10 **shepherd** *(n)* a person who looks after sheep
The ***shepherd*** must protect his sheep from the wolves.

Unit 10

1 **appoint** *(v)* to give a position to a person
The governor ***appointed*** his friend to the position.

2 **battle** *(v)* to fight
We must ***battle*** the enemy tomorrow.

3 **conquer** *(v)* to win against
The barbarians ***conquered*** the city and stole its treasures.

4 **defeat** *(v)* to beat; to win against
Our basketball team ***defeated*** the opponent tonight.

5 **dictator** *(n)* a leader with unlimited power
He rules the country like a ***dictator***.

6 **plow** *(v)* to turn over the land in a field to prepare it for planting
The farmers ***plow*** their fields in spring.

7 **prefer** *(v)* to like more than something else
Do you ***prefer*** cherries or strawberries?

8 **territory** *(n)* land that a person or country owns
How much ***territory*** does that country possess?

9 **will** *(n)* a wish; a want; a desire
My ***will*** is to be alone for a while.

10 **willingly** *(adv)* eagerly; happily
Chris went ***willingly*** with all of the others.

Unit 11

1 **ally** *(n)* a friend; a partner
The two counties signed a treaty and became ***allies***.

2 **heir** *(n)* a person who receives another's possessions when that person dies
As his father's ***heir***, Kevin received the house when his father passed away.

3 **join** *(v)* to combine; to do something with another person or group
Let's ***join*** our companies and become partners.

4 **naval** *(adj)* relating to the navy
The ***naval*** battle resulted in the sinking of several ships.

5 **nephew** *(n)* the son of one's brother or sister
My ***nephew*** Ethan is ten years old.

6 **orator** *(n)* a public speaker, often one who is very good
Perry is considered one of the great ***orators*** of this time.

7 **share** *(v)* to divided something evenly
The children decided to ***share*** the cookies.

8 **struggle** *(n)* a fight
The ***struggle*** for power lasted more than six months.

9 **talented** *(adj)* skilled; having great ability
Jenny is such a ***talented*** musician.

10 **troop** *(n)* a soldier
The general sent 1,000 ***troops*** to defend the city.

Unit 12

1 **attempt** *(v)* to try
You should ***attempt*** to call her one more time.

2 **capital** *(n)* a city in which the government of a state or country is
What is the ***capital*** of England?

3 **expand** *(v)* to become bigger in size
The president hopes to ***expand*** his company this year.

4 **historian** *(n)* a person who studies the past
Peter became a ***historian*** and studied the Roman Empire.

5 **invader** *(n)* a person who attacks others by going into their territory
The army is fighting the ***invaders*** from across the sea.

6 **remain** *(v)* to stay
We will ***remain*** in this house for as long as we can.

7 **rule** *(v)* to lead a group of people
I do not trust anyone who wants to ***rule*** others.

8 **split** *(v)* to divide evenly; to cut into two equal parts
Split the orange and share it with your sister.

9 **treasure** *(n)* something of great value
People once believed that dragons slept on big piles of ***treasure***.

10 **weak** *(adj)* having little strength or power
You need to lift weights since you are so ***weak***.

Chapter 4 Art and Artists

Unit 13

1 **adopt** *(v)* to take something and to use it as one's own
We should ***adopt*** the same methods that Richard uses.

2 **broad** *(adj)* wide
There are a ***broad*** range of methods that you can read about.

3 **brushstroke** *(n)* the movement of a brush across paper or canvas
Some artists use short ***brushstrokes*** while others use long ones.

4 **complain** *(v)* to make a negative comment about someone or something
Stop ***complaining*** and help us out.

5 **everyday** *(adj)* common; usual
Getting up in the morning is an ***everyday*** occurrence.

6 **landscape** *(n)* a picture that shows natural scenery
That artist paints so many beautiful ***landscapes***.

7 **precisely** *(adv)* exactly
Jane arrived ***precisely*** on time at three thirty.

8 **reject** *(v)* to turn down; to say no
The publisher ***rejected*** the book, but another agreed to print it.

9 **submit** *(v)* to turn in; to hand in to someone
Please ***submit*** your homework by tomorrow morning.

10 **upset** *(v)* to make angry
My friend ***upset*** me when he made a bad joke about me.

Unit 14

1 **cityscape** *(n)* a picture of a city
Walter likes to paint ***cityscapes*** in his free time.

2 **closely** *(adv)* carefully
Watch the baby ***closely*** so that she doesn't get into any trouble.

3 **genre** *(n)* a kind; a type
John's favorite movie ***genre*** is action.

4 **historical** *(adj)* relating to history
This is a work of ***historical*** fiction set in the 1800s.

5 **natural** *(adj)* good at something without having to try
He is a ***natural*** baseball player who never has to practice.

6 **noted** *(adj)* famous; well-known
Mozart is one of the most ***noted*** composers in history.

7 **portrait** *(n)* a picture of a person

They will take a family ***portrait*** later today.

8 **prolific** *(adj)* productive; producing very much

Sue is a ***prolific*** writer who has published more than twenty books.

9 **self-portrait** *(n)* a picture a person makes of him or herself

He enjoys making ***self-portraits*** in his studio.

10 **tend** *(v)* usually to do something

People ***tend*** to get sad when it rains.

Unit 15

1 **amateur** *(adj)* relating to something done by someone for fun or pleasure

The Olympics used to be only for ***amateur*** athletes.

2 **breathtaking** *(adj)* very beautiful

The view from the top of the mountain is ***breathtaking***.

3 **bronco** *(n)* a wild horse

The ***bronco*** was too wild for any cowboys to ride on it.

4 **generation** *(n)* a group of people born around the same time

The ***generation*** born in the 1940s has greatly harmed the country.

5 **instant** *(adj)* immediate; sudden

They made some ***instant*** coffee after dinner.

6 **photography** *(n)* the act of taking pictures

Photography is one of Susan's hobbies.

7 **preserve** *(v)* to save; to protect

They are trying to ***preserve*** wild elephants in Africa.

8 **professional** *(adj)* relating to something done for money

That man over there plays ***professional*** basketball.

9 **sculpt** *(v)* to make a sculpture or statue

How long does it take to ***sculpt*** a statue?

10 **sketch** *(v)* to make a quick drawing

The artist is ***sketching*** a scene by the river.

Unit 16

1 **collector** *(n)* a person who gathers things

Doug has been a stamp ***collector*** since his childhood.

2 **entire** *(adj)* complete; total

We will take a trip around the ***entire*** world next year.

3 **exhibit** *(n)* a presentation; a display

They visited the art ***exhibit*** at the museum.

4 **gallery** *(n)* a place that sells or displays art

I bought a work of art from the ***gallery*** downtown.

5 **hometown** *(n)* the place where a person was born or grew up

Tom's ***hometown*** is a small place in Texas.

6 **loan** *(v)* to lend; to let someone borrow something

The bank will ***loan*** the company one million dollars.

7 **masterpiece** *(n)* a great work of art

She considers this work to be her ***masterpiece***.

8 **permanent** *(adj)* forever

Do not use ***permanent*** ink, or else you will never be able to erase it.

9 **still-life** *(n)* a painting of objects that do not move

This painting is a ***still-life*** showing fruit in a bowl.

10 **vibrant** *(adj)* colorful; alive

This is one of the most ***vibrant*** communities in the city.

Chapter 5 The Environment

Unit 17

1 **farmer** *(n)* a person who grows crops or raises animals
His grandfather is a ***farmer*** who grows potatoes and tomatoes.

2 **fertilizer** *(n)* chemicals that improve the quality of soil
We use ***fertilizer*** to help our crops grow better.

3 **landfill** *(n)* a garbage dump; a place where people put their garbage
There is a terrible smell coming from the ***landfill***.

4 **mass** *(adj)* affecting a large number of people
Mass media has the ability to reach large numbers of people.

5 **miner** *(n)* a person who digs in the ground for ore or precious metals
The ***miners*** were happy when they found some diamonds.

6 **pollute** *(v)* to make dirty or unclean
The factories in the city are ***polluting*** the air.

7 **reduce** *(v)* to lower; to lessen
Try to ***reduce*** the amount of garbage you create.

8 **release** *(v)* to let go
The fishermen always ***release*** the fish that they catch.

9 **unhealthy** *(adj)* harmful; not nutritious
It is ***unhealthy*** to eat too much fast food.

10 **waterway** *(n)* a body of water that ships travel on
The Panama Canal is one of the Earth's most important ***waterways***.

Unit 18

1 **abiotic** *(adj)* not alive; relating to objects that are not alive
Abiotic resources exist in great amounts on the Earth.

2 **abundant** *(adj)* plentiful; existing in great amounts
The farmer owns an ***abundant*** amount of land.

3 **biotic** *(adj)* living; relating to life
Biotic resources include plants and animals.

4 **conserve** *(v)* to save; to preserve
They hope to ***conserve*** the forest so that it is not cut down.

5 **declare** *(v)* to state out loud
He ***declared*** that he was the best player in the league.

6 **environmentalist** *(n)* a person who takes care of the environment
The ***environmentalists*** hope to reduce the amount of pollution.

7 **improve** *(v)* to get better
Try to ***improve*** so that your next test is better.

8 **supply** *(n)* an amount of something
The soldiers have a large ***supply*** of bullets.

9 **valuable** *(adj)* worth a lot of money
That is one of the most ***valuable*** paintings in the world.

10 **vast** *(adj)* very large; enormous; extensive
The field covers a ***vast*** area of land.

Unit 19

1 **benefit** *(n)* an advantage; a good point
Name some ***benefits*** of going on this trip.

2 **collect** *(v)* to gather; to bring together
Let's ***collect*** as much trash as we can from the park.

3 **glossware** *(n)* containers that are made of glass
That company makes expensive ***glassware.***

4 **leak** *(v)* to escape, like a liquid from a container
There is some water ***leaking*** from the pot.

5 **logo** *(n)* a symbol that represents a country, company, or group
What is the ***logo*** of that company?

6 **loop** *(n)* a ring; a circle
The highway forms a ***loop*** around the entire city.

7 **recyclable** *(adj)* able to be used again
Are these plastic containers ***recyclable***?

8 **sort** *(v)* to divide into different categories
We must ***sort*** these objects according to what they are made of.

9 **stage** *(n)* a step in a larger process
The first ***stage*** is for us to raise some money.

10 **support** *(n)* care; backing
The group needs the ***support*** of more of its members.

Unit 20

1 **cheap** *(adj)* inexpensive; not costing a lot of money
A meal at that restaurant is very ***cheap***.

2 **cloudy** *(adj)* having many clouds in the sky
On ***cloudy*** days, the sun does not shine much.

3 **decrease** *(v)* to do down; to become lower
Please ***decrease*** the volume on the TV.

4 **fragile** *(adj)* easily broken or upset
This object is ***fragile***, so do not drop it.

5 **harm** *(v)* to hurt; to damage
The dog ***hurt*** its leg while it was playing outside.

6 **inefficient** *(adj)* not operating or running well
This is an ***inefficient*** way to run a business.

7 **maintenance** *(n)* care for something, often mechanical; upkeep
The ***maintenance*** of the computers is very important.

8 **practical** *(adj)* useful; real
Show me a ***practical*** use of this object.

9 **tidal** *(adj)* relating to the tides in the ocean
Some countries are starting to create electricity from ***tidal*** power.

10 **upriver** *(n)* an area located close to a river's source
We sailed our boat ***upriver***.

Memo

memo

memo

A Guide to Mastering Listening Skills for Academic Lectures

Mastering Listening Skills

Michael A. Putlack

1

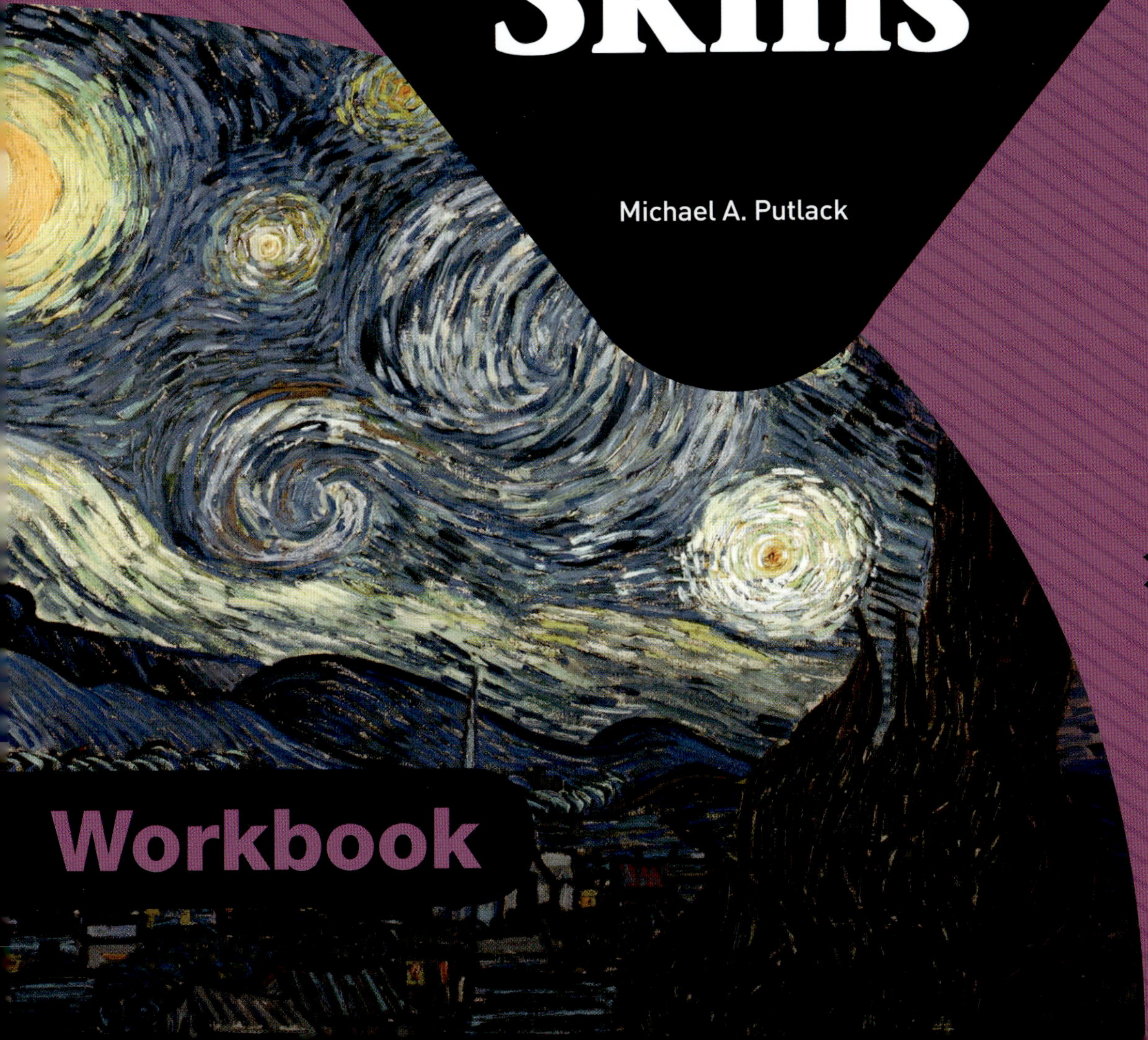

Workbook

DARAKWON

Mastering Listening Skills

Workbook

1

DARAKWON

Chapter

1

Natural Disasters

Unit 01 Krakatoa

A Listen to the talk on page 12 again. Then, write the answers to the questions.

1 What can volcanoes spew when they erupt?

____

2 When did Krakatoa erupt?

____

3 What happened to the island of Rakata when Krakatoa erupted?

____

4 From how far away did people hear the eruption of Krakatoa?

____

5 How did the eruption of Krakatoa affect sunrises around the world?

____

B Use the words in the box to complete the sentences. You may need to change the forms of the words.

spew	dormant	destructive	natural disaster	faraway place

1 That is a ______________ volcano which has not erupted in 1,000 years.

2 I want to visit a ______________ for my next vacation.

3 The volcano will ______________ a lot of ash when it erupts.

4 Have you ever been in a ______________ like an earthquake?

5 The eruption was so ______________ that the entire town was covered with lava.

C Listen to the talk on page 14 again. Then, answer T (true) or F (false).

1 _______ Krakatoa was the most powerful volcanic eruption in history.

2 _______ The eruption of Krakatoa damaged the islands around it.

3 _______ A new island called Anak Krakatoa arose in 1927.

4 _______ Anak Krakatoa is 3,000 meters high today.

5 _______ Anak Krakatoa erupted and killed 100,000 people.

D Listen to the talk. Then, write C (cause) or E (effect) for each sentence.

Notes

1 _______ The size of the island of Hawaii is increasing.

2 _______ Kilauea started its current eruption in 1983.

3 _______ The lava coming out of the volcano destroys anything it touches.

Unit 02

The San Francisco Earthquake

A Listen to the talk on page 16 again. Then, write the answers to the questions.

1 Where is San Francisco?

____

2 When did the San Francisco Earthquake happen?

____

3 How big was the earthquake?

____

4 What caused the most destruction in San Francisco?

____

5 Around how many people died after the event?

____

B Use the words in the box to complete the sentences. You may need to change the forms of the words.

gas line	tremor	homeless	last	Richter scale

1 Scientists use the ______________ to measure the strength of earthquakes.

2 I smell gas, so there may be a leak in the ______________.

3 They felt sorry for the ______________ man living under the bridge.

4 Do you know how long the game is going to ______________?

5 The last ______________ was not as powerful as the first earthquake.

C Listen to the talk on page 18 again. Then, circle the correct answers.

1 The student's (report / science project) is on the New Madrid Earthquake.

2 There were (two / three) strong earthquakes before the New Madrid Earthquake happened.

3 New Madrid is located in the state of (Mississippi / Missouri).

4 After the earthquake, some new (lakes / rivers) formed.

5 The Mississippi River began to flow (north / south) after the New Madrid Earthquake.

D Listen to the talk. Then, write C (cause) or E (effect) for each sentence.

Notes

1 ______ The World Series was delayed by ten days.

2 ______ Thousands of people were hurt, and more than sixty people were killed.

3 ______ A powerful earthquake happened right before a baseball game began.

Unit 03

The Tunguska Event

A Listen to the talk on page 20 again. Then, write the answers to the questions.

1 How big are most of the meteors that enter the Earth's atmosphere?

____

2 How large was the meteor that hit Tunguska?

____

3 How powerful was the meteor when it exploded?

____

4 How bright was the meteor when it exploded?

____

5 What do many astronomers do now because of the Tunguska Event?

____

B Use the words in the box to complete the sentences. You may need to change the forms of the words.

remote area	blow up	forested area	atomic bomb	populated region

1 Be careful handling the bomb, or it may ____________.

2 An ____________ is the most powerful weapon that country has.

3 Seoul is the most ____________ in all of Korea.

4 The farmer is happy living in a ____________ away from most people.

5 This ____________ of the country has countless trees.

C Listen to the talk on page 22 again. Then, choose the correct answers.

1 Dinosaurs were the ________________ animals on the Earth for millions of years.

ⓐ smallest ⓑ dominant ⓒ only

2 When the dinosaurs died, the age of ________________ began.

ⓐ lizards ⓑ birds ⓒ mammals

3 An asteroid hit the Yucatan Peninsula around ________________ million years ago.

ⓐ 6 ⓑ 60 ⓒ 65

4 The ________________ from the asteroid kept the sun from shining on most of the planet.

ⓐ dust ⓑ fire ⓒ clouds

5 The ________________ went extinct because of the cold temperatures.

ⓐ dinosaurs ⓑ animals ⓒ birds

D Listen to the talk. Then, choose the correct connecting words for the sentences.

Notes

1 A bright light streaked across the sky. (Then / Finally), it exploded.

2 The explosion caused the meteor to break apart, (because / so) numerous fireballs fell to the Earth.

3 More than 1,000 people were hurt by the explosion, (and / but) no one was killed.

Unit 04 The Southeast Asian Tsunami

A Listen to the talk on page 24 again. Then, write the answers to the questions.

1 What can create a tsunami?

___

2 How high can tsunamis be?

___

3 How powerful was the earthquake that caused the Southeast Asian Tsunami?

___

4 How many people died because of the Southeast Asian Tsunami?

___

5 What did people around the world do after the Southeast Asian Tsunami?

___

B Use the words in the box to complete the sentences. You may need to change the forms of the words.

be wiped out	incredibly	fast-moving	survivor	aid

1 Many charity groups ___ poor people and the homeless.

2 His village ___ by the tsunami last year.

3 There was only one ___ of the plane crash.

4 Tim is ___ intelligent, but he does not always work hard.

5 I can see a ___ object flying in the sky.

C Listen to the talk on page 26 again. Then, fill in the blanks with the correct words.

1 There was an ________________ earthquake in Japan on March 11, 2011.

2 The earthquake caused many tsunamis that hit the east ________________ of Japan.

3 ________________ of people died because of the tsunamis.

4 The tsunamis hit several ________________ reactors.

5 Officials are concerned about the nuclear power plant in ________________.

D Listen to the talk. Then, choose the correct connecting words for the sentences.

Notes

1 The eruption destroyed more than half of the island. (Because / In addition), it caused many tsunamis.

2 The Minoan Civilization existed on Crete. (However / Therefore), the tsunami hit Crete and killed many people.

3 Atlantis was the greatest civilization in ancient times. (So / But) it sank beneath the ocean.

Chapter

2

Fantasy Worlds

Unit 05

Narnia

A **Listen to the talk on page 30 again. Then, write the answers to the questions.**

1 How do the four children enter Narnia?

____

2 What can many of the animals in Narnia do?

____

3 What did the White Witch do to Narnia?

____

4 Who wrote *The Lion, the Witch, and the Wardrobe*?

____

5 How many books are there in *The Chronicles of Narnia*?

____

B **Use the words in the box to complete the sentences. You may need to change the forms of the words.**

centaur	beloved	find out	chronicle	fantasy world

1 A ______________ has the body of a horse but the upper body of a man.

2 Let's try to ______________ the answer to the question.

3 The writer hopes to create a ______________ to set stories in.

4 Jenny is the ______________ daughter of the mayor of the city.

5 During his time as a soldier, Rick wrote a ______________ about the battles he fought in.

C Listen to the talk on page 32 again. Then, answer T (true) or F (false).

1 ______ Mr. Tumnus is a faun.

2 ______ Mr. Tumnus tells the White Witch about Lucy.

3 ______ Reepicheep is the leader of the talking hamsters.

4 ______ Reepicheep appears in the book *Prince Caspian*.

5 ______ There are many funny scenes with Reepicheep in the books.

D Listen to the talk. Then, write T (true) or F (false) for the following statements about *The Chronicles of Narnia*.

Notes

1 ______ *The Magician's Nephew* describes the creation of Narnia.

2 ______ Queen Jadis appears in the book *The Last Battle*.

3 ______ Many characters go to Aslan's Country at the end of *The Last Battle*.

Unit 06

Middle-Earth

A **Listen to the talk on page 34 again. Then, write the answers to the questions.**

1 Who created Middle-earth?

____

2 What kinds of creatures are there in Middle-earth?

____

3 What was the first book about Middle-earth?

____

4 What are the best-known books about Middle-earth?

____

5 What is the quest in these books?

____

B **Use the words in the box to complete the sentences. You may need to change the forms of the words.**

overcome	humanlike	epic tale	wizard	best-known

1 The ______________ philosopher from ancient times is Plato.

2 Hobbits are ______________ creatures but are very short.

3 Gandalf is the greatest ______________ in all of Middle-earth.

4 We must ______________ all of our problems in order to succeed.

5 She is currently writing an ______________ set in a fantasy world.

C Listen to the talk on page 36 again. Then, circle the correct answers.

1 The third movie in *The Lord of the Rings* trilogy is (*The Two Towers* / *The Return of the King*).

2 The student thinks the movie is one of the (best / worst) movies he has ever seen.

3 There are (two / three) stories in the movie.

4 Frodo Baggins and Samwise Gamgee go into Mordor to (find / destroy) the One Ring.

5 The second story involves armies fighting the forces of the evil (Gandalf / Sauron).

D Listen to the talk. Then, write T (true) or F (false) for the following statements about *The Hobbit*.

Notes

1 ______ Bilbo Baggins, Gandalf, and some dwarves go to the Lonely Mountain.

2 ______ Smaug stole the treasure from the dwarves.

3 ______ Bilbo Baggins shoots Smaug with an arrow and kills the dragon.

Unit 07

The Magical World of Oz

A Listen to the talk on page 38 again. Then, write the answers to the questions.

1 Who starred in the movie *The Wizard of Oz*?

____

2 Who wrote the book *The Wonderful Wizard of Oz*?

____

3 Why are the Munchkins happy to meet Dorothy?

____

4 Where is Dorothy going when she meets the Scarecrow, Tin Woodman, and Cowardly Lion?

____

5 What happens to Dorothy and Toto at the end of the book?

____

B Use the words in the box to complete the sentences. You may need to change the forms of the words.

hit	deal with	title	make friends with	pick up

1 It is easy for children to _______________ others.

2 That movie was a big _______________ and made millions of dollars.

3 Can you please _______________ the books from the floor?

4 I cannot remember the _______________ of the movie I just saw.

5 We need to _______________ some problems before we go out.

C Listen to the talk on page 40 again. Then, choose the correct answers.

1 Ursula Le Guin wrote the book ________________.

ⓐ *A Magician of Earthsea* ⓑ *A Wizard of Earthsea* ⓒ *A Witch of Earthsea*

2 There are a total of ________________ books about Earthsea.

ⓐ five ⓑ six ⓒ seven

3 The land in Earthsea is made up of ________________.

ⓐ deserts ⓑ forests ⓒ islands

4 Earthsea is a place where people can use ________________.

ⓐ magic ⓑ technology ⓒ knowledge

5 The wizard ________________ is one of the main characters in the books.

ⓐ Jasper ⓑ Ogion ⓒ Ged

D Listen to the talk. Then, answer the question.

Notes

What can be inferred about the Wizard of Oz?

ⓐ He is braver than the Cowardly Lion.

ⓑ He does not have any magical power.

ⓒ He becomes friends with Dorothy.

Unit 08 The World of *Harry Potter*

A Listen to the talk on page 42 again. Then, write the answers to the questions.

1 Who is fighting the war in the *Harry Potter* books?

____

2 How many books are in the *Harry Potter* series?

____

3 Who wrote the *Harry Potter* books?

____

4 What is the name of Harry Potter's school?

____

5 Who is the evil wizard that Harry Potter fights?

____

B Use the words in the box to complete the sentences. You may need to change the forms of the words.

battle	evil	billion	skill	all sorts of

1 There are more than two ____________ people living in Asia.

2 The magician can do ____________ magic tricks.

3 A famous ____________ was fought here many years ago.

4 It takes a lot of ____________ to be able to program a computer.

5 There are some ____________ men who want to cause harm to others.

C Listen to the talk on page 44 again. Then, fill in the blanks with the correct words.

1 Jim Butcher is the author of the ________________ series *The Dresden Files*.

2 Harry Dresden is a wizard and ________________.

3 There are ________________ books in the series right now.

4 Harry gains more and more ________________ as the books proceed.

5 Harry has to fights many monsters as well as strange beings called ________________.

D Listen to the talk. Then, answer the question.

Notes

What can be inferred about Harry Potter?

ⓐ There are many myths about him around the world.

ⓑ Joseph Campbell wrote a book about him.

ⓒ His story is similar to other stories people tell.

Chapter

3

The Roman Era

Unit 09 Romulus and Remus

A Listen to the talk on page 48 again. Then, write the answers to the questions.

1 When was Rome founded?

____

2 What was the name of Numitor's daughter?

____

3 Who was the father of Romulus and Remus?

____

4 What did the woodpecker do for Romulus and Remus?

____

5 Where did Romulus and Remus decide to build their own city?

____

B Use the words in the box to complete the sentences. You may need to change the forms of the words.

found	inherit	send away	float off	give birth to

1 The woman will ______________ a baby boy later this month.

2 Jack will ______________ one million dollars from his parents.

3 The balloon looks like it will ______________ into the sky.

4 She wants to ______________ a charity to help others.

5 Please ______________ the food because I am not hungry.

C **Listen to the talk on page 50 again. Then, answer T (true) or F (false).**

1 ______ The Greek Homer wrote the *Iliad* and *Odyssey*.

2 ______ Virgil was the Greek poet who wrote the *Aeneid*.

3 ______ Aeneas and his followers escaped from the city of Troy.

4 ______ Aeneas married Queen Dido of Carthage.

5 ______ Aeneas married Lavinia but was killed by Turnus.

D **Listen to the talk. Then, put the sentences in chronological order.**

Notes

1 ______ Cupid scratched himself with an arrow and fell in love with Psyche.

2 ______ People worshipped Psyche because she was so beautiful.

3 ______ Venus was jealous, so she sent Cupid to punish Psyche.

Unit 10

The Roman Republic

A Listen to the talk on page 52 again. Then, write the answers to the questions.

1 How long did kings rule Rome?

____

2 When did Rome become a republic?

____

3 What did the Roman senators do?

____

4 Who did Rome fight in the Punic Wars?

____

5 When did the Roman Republic end?

____

B Use the words in the box to complete the sentences. You may need to change the forms of the words.

wealthy aristocrat	stabilize	peninsula	expand	come into conflict with

1 Korea is a _______________ because it is surrounded by water on three sides.

2 The company wants to _______________ so that it can make more money.

3 The _______________ gave all of his money to the poor.

4 The two countries often _______________ each other, so they have fought several wars.

5 We must _______________ the situation, or many people will get hurt.

C Listen to the talk on page 54 again. Then, circle the correct answers.

1 Cincinnatus was a Roman (senator / consul) in 460 B.C.

2 Cincinnatus preferred to spend time (on his farm / at his city home).

3 The Roman Senate was worried about the (Aequi / Trojans).

4 The Roman Senate offered to make Cincinnatus (king / dictator).

5 Cincinnatus (gave up / kept) power after he defeated the enemy army.

D Listen to the talk. Then, write the correct times in the blanks in the sentences and put them in chronological order.

Notes

1 ______ Hannibal fought the Battle of Zama in ________________ and lost to the Romans.

2 ______ In ________________, a huge Roman army was destroyed at the Battle of Cannae.

3 ______ Hannibal crossed the Alps and defeated the Romans at Trebia in ________________.

Unit 11 Julius Caesar

A **Listen to the talk on page 56 again. Then, write the answers to the questions.**

1 When was Julius Caesar born?

____

2 What caused the Roman Republic to go into decline?

____

3 Which region did Julius Caesar become the governor of?

____

4 Why was the Roman Senate worried about Julius Caesar?

____

5 When was Julius Caesar killed?

____

B **Use the words in the box to complete the sentences. You may need to change the forms of the words.**

be accomplished	go into decline	gain power	general	be in charge of

1 George is ambitious and wants to ______________ at his company.

2 The country began to ______________ because its politicians were so corrupt.

3 Lucy ______________ the department, so please listen to her.

4 ______________ Sherman was one of the greatest military leaders in history.

5 David ______________ at sports and is going to play professional baseball.

C Listen to the talk on page 58 again. Then, choose the correct answers.

1 There was a struggle for power in ________________ after Julius Caesar was killed.

ⓐ Rome ⓑ Carthage ⓒ Greece

2 The time after Caesar's death was called the ________________.

ⓐ First Triumvirate ⓑ Second Triumvirate ⓒ Third Triumvirate

3 The army of ________________ fought and defeated the army of Lepidus.

ⓐ Octavian ⓑ Mark Antony ⓒ Brutus

4 Mark Antony joined forces with ________________ in Egypt.

ⓐ Tutankhamen ⓑ Ramses ⓒ Cleopatra

5 Octavian defeated Mark Antony at the Battle of ________________ in 31 B.C.

ⓐ Cairo ⓑ Actium ⓒ Alexandria

D Listen to the talk. Then, match the sentences to find the problem and the solutions.

Notes

1 Much of Rome burned in a fire, ⓐ so they rebelled and ended his reign.

2 Agrippina made Nero upset, ⓑ but Nero only helped the people a little.

3 The Romans turned against Nero, ⓒ so he had his mother executed.

Unit 12 The Fall of the Roman Empire

A Listen to the talk on page 60 again. Then, write the answers to the questions.

1 What did Diocletian do to the Roman Empire?

____

2 What barbarian tribes gained power in the west?

____

3 How were the politicians in Rome?

____

4 When did a Germanic army first invade Rome?

____

5 Who was the leader of the Germanic army in 476?

____

B Use the words in the box to complete the sentences. You may need to change the forms of the words.

a great deal	give up the throne	harm	be the case	legion

1 The Roman ____________ defeated the enemy and captured the city.

2 I have ____________ of time, so we can talk for a while.

3 Sue suffered some ____________ when she was in a car accident.

4 That ____________ for John, who is working hard right now.

5 The king decided to ____________ to marry a commoner.

C Listen to the talk on page 62 again. Then, fill in the blanks with the correct words.

1 ________________ was the first Byzantine emperor.

2 The capital of the Byzantine Empire was ________________.

3 The Byzantine Empire lasted until the year ________________.

4 The Byzantine Empire often fought wars against ________________ invaders.

5 An army of ________________ captured Constantinople and ended the Byzantine Empire.

D Listen to the talk. Then, write P (problem) or S (solution).

Notes

1 ______ Belisarius and Narses recaptured much of the land.

2 ______ Justinian improve the law by making the Justinian Code.

3 ______ The Byzantine Empire had lost a lot of land in the past.

Chapter

4

Art and Artists

Unit 13 Realism

A **Listen to the talk on page 66 again. Then, write the answers to the questions.**

1 What did the art of the Romantic Era stress?

____

2 When did the Realism style last from?

____

3 What did Realist artists paint pictures of?

____

4 How did Realist artists want to show the world?

____

5 Who were three famous Realist artists?

____

B **Use the words in the box to complete the sentences. You may need to change the forms of the words.**

lower class	upper class	influence	pay attention to	art critic

1 Most members of the ______________ have a lot of money.

2 ______________ the teacher, or you will not understand the lesson.

3 The ______________ liked the paintings by the new artist very much.

4 That poor family belongs to the ______________.

5 Many teachers are able to ______________ the lives of their students.

C Listen to the talk on page 68 again. Then, answer T (true) or F (false).

1 ______ Edouard Manet wanted to be a doctor when he was young.

2 ______ An early painting by Manet was *The Absinthe Drinker*.

3 ______ The Salon was the official art exhibition of England.

4 ______ Manet began to use bright colors like the Impressionists.

5 ______ Manet never became a famous painter during his life.

D Listen to the talk. Then, choose the correct summary sentence.

Notes

ⓐ Winslow Homer was mostly known for his illustrations and sketches.
ⓑ Winslow Homer created several kinds of art during his life.
ⓒ Winslow Homer was the greatest artist in American history.

Unit 14 Dutch Golden Age Painting

A **Listen to the talk on page 70 again. Then, write the answers to the questions.**

1 When did the Netherlands become very wealthy and powerful?

____

2 How many paintings did Dutch artists produce during the Dutch Golden Age?

____

3 What kinds of paintings did Dutch artists make?

____

4 Who was the most famous artist during the Dutch Golden Age?

____

5 Who were three other noted artists from that time?

____

B **Use the words in the box to complete the sentences. You may need to change the forms of the words.**

global empire	still-life	striking	master painter	art historian

1 Britain once had a ________________ that made it incredibly powerful.

2 He was a ________________, so his works sell for millions of dollars today.

3 If you want to be an ________________, you must study for a long time.

4 She is a ________________ young woman who impresses everyone with her beauty.

5 The ________________ is a painting of some flowers in a vase.

C Listen to the talk on page 72 again. Then, circle the correct answers.

1 Rembrandt van Rijn is one of the best-known (Dutch / French) artists.

2 Rembrandt made more than (60 / 600) paintings during his life.

3 Rembrandt loved to paint (landscapes / portraits).

4 Many of Rembrandt's paintings had (religious / funny) themes.

5 *The Night Watch* is (an enormous / a tiny) painting that Rembrandt made.

D Listen to the talk. Then, choose the correct summary sentence.

Notes

ⓐ Most of the paintings of Johannes Vermeer use dark colors.

ⓑ Johannes Vermeer painted the masterpiece *The Girl with a Pearl Earring*.

ⓒ Johannes Vermeer was a great artist from the Dutch Golden Age.

Unit 15

Frederic Remington

A Listen to the talk on page 74 again. Then, write the answers to the questions.

1 Where did most Americans live in the 1800s?

____

2 What animals lived in the western part of the country?

____

3 What did Frederic Remington start doing in his early twenties?

____

4 What did Frederic Remington paint with?

____

5 What is the name of the Remington sculpture that is in the Oval Office?

____

B Use the words in the box to complete the sentences. You may need to change the forms of the words.

fascinating	cowboy	be intrigued by	settlers	cavalry

1 I ______________ the thought of moving to another country.

2 The ______________ chose to live in a dangerous area.

3 Bill is a ______________ who spends his time ranching cattle.

4 The ______________ arrived just in time to fight the Indians that had attacked the town.

5 It is ______________ how the artist creates such beautiful pictures on canvas.

C Listen to the talk on page 76 again. Then, choose the correct answers.

1 ________________ involves making works of art with a camera.

ⓐ Picture ⓑ Photography ⓒ Photos

2 Ansel Adams visited ________________ National Park when he was a teenager.

ⓐ Yosemite ⓑ Yellowstone ⓒ Grand Canyon

3 Ansel Adams worked to help ________________ the park during his life.

ⓐ preserve ⓑ respect ⓒ manage

4 Ansel Adams later became a ________________ photographer.

ⓐ amateur ⓑ semipro ⓒ professional

5 Ansel Adams often used ________________ film to take pictures.

ⓐ black-and-white ⓑ sepia tone ⓒ color

D Listen to the talk. Take notes on the topics written below.

Notes

1 upstate New York: ________________________________

2 types of paintings: ________________________________

3 Hudson River School artists: ________________________________

Unit 16

Vincent van Gogh

A **Listen to the talk on page 78 again. Then, write the answers to the questions.**

1 How many paintings did Vincent van Gogh sell during his life?

____

2 How did Vincent van Gogh get money?

____

3 How did Vincent van Gogh die?

____

4 What was Vincent van Gogh's first major work?

____

5 How did Vincent van Gogh's style change later in his life?

____

B **Use the words in the box to complete the sentences. You may need to change the forms of the words.**

commit suicide	formal training	commercial	mental illness	recognizable

1 Even though she has no ____________, she is an amazing musician.

2 Joe suffers from a ____________, so he takes medicine every day.

3 Life is always worth living, so it is a mistake to ____________.

4 The queen is one of the most ____________ people in the world.

5 The new product was popular and became a ____________ success.

C Listen to the talk on page 80 again. Then, fill in the blanks with the correct words.

1 The Vincent van Gogh Museum is located in ________________ in the Netherlands.

2 The museum has more than ________________ paintings by van Gogh in its permanent collection.

3 The museum also has many of van Gogh's ________________ and drawings.

4 Some museums and collectors ________________ the museum other works by van Gogh.

5 The works are from every ________________ in van Gogh's career.

D Listen to the talk. Take notes on the topics written below.

Notes

1 *Starry Night*: ____

2 the night sky: ____

3 the town: ____

Chapter

5

The Environment

Unit 17 Pollution

A Listen to the talk on page 84 again. Then, write the answers to the questions.

1 What are the three main types of pollution?

____

2 What are two major sources of air pollution?

____

3 How does water pollution affect fish?

____

4 How do farmers cause soil pollution?

____

5 What are landfills?

____

B Use the words in the box to complete the sentences. You may need to change the forms of the words.

insecticide	harmful	dump	breathe	water source

1 Smoking can be ______________ to your health.

2 You should not ______________ your garbage into the river.

3 Every human on the planet needs to ______________ oxygen to survive.

4 Because of the drought, people needed to look for a new ______________.

5 The farmer needs to use ______________ to protect his crops.

C Listen to the talk on page 86 again. Then, answer T (true) or F (false).

1 ______ There are many ways humans can improve the environment.

2 ______ Cars and buses create a lot of pollution.

3 ______ Electric cars pollute the air more than gas-powered cars.

4 ______ Water pollution is a small problem nowadays.

5 ______ Reducing the number of oil spills can reduce water pollution.

D Listen to the talk. Then, complete the classification chart about nuclear power plants.

Notes

Nuclear Power Plants

- Are very ⓐ ______________
- Are not like the nuclear reactor at Chernobyl in ⓑ ______________
- Won't release ⓒ ______________ into the air, ground, or water
- Don't pollute ⓓ ______________
- Can create a great amount of ⓔ ______________

Unit 18

Natural Resources

A **Listen to the talk on page 88 again. Then, write the answers to the questions.**

1 What is a biotic resource?

____

2 What is a renewable resource?

____

3 Why are animals renewable resources?

____

4 What kind of resource are fossil fuels?

____

5 Why should people conserve metals such as gold, silver, and iron?

____

B **Use the words in the box to complete the sentences. You may need to change the forms of the words.**

finite supply	rare metal	endless	primary	reproduce

1 What is the ________________ subject that you want to study?

2 There is a ________________ of coal and oil.

3 Most animals ________________ once a year.

4 Platinum is an extremely valuable ________________.

5 The galaxy is so big that it appears ________________.

C Listen to the talk on page 90 again. Then, circle the correct answers.

1 Environmentalists claim that the Earth is running out of (fossil fuels / water).

2 The environmentalists are (right / wrong) about their claim.

3 (Geologists / Geographers) are discovering new oil fields all over the Earth.

4 There are many big oil fields deep beneath the (Arctic / Atlantic) Ocean.

5 It is now possible to remove oil from (oil sands / oil pits).

D Listen to the talk. Then, complete the classification chart about fracking.

Notes

Fracking

- Is a method to get ⓐ ______________
- ⓑ ______________ beneath the surface
- ⓒ ______________ fracking fluid into the ground
- Gets the natural gas to the surface
- Is very common in ⓓ ______________
- Is helping the United States become ⓔ ______________

Unit 19 Recycling

A Listen to the talk on page 92 again. Then, write the answers to the questions.

1 What kinds of objects can people recycle?

____

2 How does recycling benefit natural resources?

____

3 What is a benefit of recycling paper?

____

4 What is a problem at many landfills?

____

5 What is a problem with electronics and batteries?

____

B Use the words in the box to complete the sentences. You may need to change the forms of the words.

set aside	textile	precious	dispose of	mine

1 The _______________ factory outside the city makes all kinds of clothes.

2 Please _______________ this item by putting it in the garbage can.

3 The company hired more people to _______________ silver.

4 We should _______________ this item so that we can use it later.

5 Wendy's diamond ring is her most _______________ possession.

C Listen to the talk on page 94 again. Then, choose the correct answers.

1 The recycling logo has three ______________ arrows on it.

ⓐ blue ⓑ green ⓒ orange

2 The logo is called the Recycling ______________.

ⓐ Oval ⓑ Circle ⓒ Loop

3 The first stage is ______________.

ⓐ collecting ⓑ considering ⓒ comparing

4 In the processing stage, the items are ______________ according to what they are made of.

ⓐ sorted ⓑ registered ⓒ regarded

5 The final stage involves people ______________ recycled items.

ⓐ looking at ⓑ buying ⓒ making

D Listen to the talk. Then, answer the question.

Notes

Why does the speaker mention the Internet?

ⓐ To give the listeners the address of a website

ⓑ To say that people can learn about recycling on it

ⓐ To encourage the listeners to look for some websites

Unit 20

Renewable Energy

A **Listen to the talk on page 96 again. Then, write the answers to the questions.**

1 What percentage of the world's energy needs do fossil fuels provide?

____

2 What are some types of renewable energy?

____

3 Where does hydroelectric power come from?

____

4 How clean is renewable energy?

____

5 What is a problem with wind turbines?

____

B **Use the words in the box to complete the sentences. You may need to change the forms of the words.**

turn to	fossil fuel	ocean tides	efficient	wind turbines

1 Coal is the most common ______________ in this country.

2 ______________ can create large amounts of electricity in some places.

3 There are many ______________ that produce energy when the wind blows.

4 Let's ______________ another method and see if it will work.

5 You must be more ______________ with your time to be more productive.

C Listen to the talk on page 98 again. Then, fill in the blanks with the correct words.

1 There is a ________________ power plant at the dam.

2 The dam provides both cheap and ________________ electricity.

3 The electric bills of local residents have ________________ since the dam opened.

4 The dam does not ________________ the air at all.

5 There are some ________________ for salmon to use to get upriver.

D Listen to the talk. Then, answer the question.

Notes

Why does the speaker discuss the Sahara Desert?

ⓐ To talk about the weather that it gets

ⓑ To mention where it is located

ⓒ To describe a solar power project there

memo

memo

We Bring You the World

Mastering Listening Skills Book 1

Mastering Listening Skills Book 1 has several objectives. First, it will help learners improve their English abilities, particularly their listening skills. Next, it will teach them valuable knowledge about a wide range of academic topics. The talks themselves will also entertain learners as they listen to them. Finally, *Mastering Listening Skills Book 1* will help learners prepare for various standardized tests that they may take in the future. For instance, many questions about the talks are similar to those that appear on the iBT TOEFL® Junior and iBT TOEFL® exams. So, by using this book, learners should be able to get higher scores on the tests they take in the future.

For Basic-Level Listeners

Developing Listening Skills Book 1
Developing Listening Skills Book 2

For Intermediate-Level Listeners

Mastering Listening Skills Book 1
Mastering Listening Skills Book 2

Special Features

- **Academic and Entertaining Listening Talks**
  Contains 20 listening talks on all kinds of academic subjects
- **Listening Comprehension and Vocabulary Review Questions**
  Lets listeners test their comprehension of the talks
- **Useful Listening Skills**
  Teaches listeners important skills to make them better at listening
- **Detailed Word List**
  Provides definitions and sample sentences of difficult vocabulary words
- **Comprehensive Workbook**
  Contains extra questions, vocabulary exercises, and listening skill exercises
- **Recordings of Listening Talks**
  Lets listeners improve their listening and pronunciation skills by listening to native speakers